JUST OFF THE STREETCAR LINE©
(a New Orleans melodrama)

Margrete Grey Wolf

JUST OFF THE STREETCAR LINE©
(a New Orleans melodrama)

by Margrete Grey Wolf

This book is dedicated to all the wonderful people who live in the neighborhoods of New Orleans. God bless them all.

Copyright © 2005 by Margrete Grey Wolf

Cover photo by Running Bear
Book design by Margrete Grey Wolf

All rights reserved. No part of this work may be reproduced or transmitted in any form or by any means, electronic or mechanical, including photocopying or recording, or by any information storage or retrieval system without prior written permission from the publisher. Manufactured in the United States of America.

NeutralGround Publications, L.L.C.
2321 Short Street
New Orleans, LA 70118

ISBN 0-9743609-8-8

This book is a work of fiction. All names and characters are either invented or used fictitiously. The events described are imaginary. If you recognize yourself among the characters of this book, then truth is indeed stranger than fiction.

ACKNOWLEDGEMENTS

It truly takes a village to publish a book, and I would like to thank all those people in my little village of friends, family and colleagues for their help and support. First of all, I must give a heartfelt thanks to my wonderful husband Bear, the best person I know, for being there for me every step of the way and without whose help this book would have never been published much less distributed. I also want to thank Byron, who went above and beyond in his role as Computer Wizard; Heidi, for the equipment and advice; Ashley, for paving the way; Yvonne, my dear friend who has been in my corner since 1987, rain or shine; Rob, my oldest friend, who picked me up off the floor and fed me tacos more times than I care to remember; Norma, for her encouragement and friendship; my *fabu* friend Leo, for being such a bright light in my life; Hazel, for your support and friendship over the years; my dear son Samuel for his marketing assistance; and to Nathalie and Randi, my lovely European friends and cheerleaders. And to all other friends who leant verbal and moral support throughout this endeavor, you know who you are and I thank you.

FOREWORD

Heard in line at Galatoire's:
"God created New Orleans. The Devil made Baton Rouge."

New Orleans is an antique city composed of antique neighborhoods. (We used to think we were just an old city full of elderly neighborhoods, but we discovered some years ago that the word "antique" sells better and we have been using it ever since.) The St. Charles streetcar line runs from Canal Street and St. Charles Avenue downtown all the way out to Carrollton and Claiborne Avenues way uptown past Tulane University. The streetcar is not just some quaint method of travel to delight the tourists; it is an important mode of daily transportation for many locals who live near the streetcar line, invaluable to those of us who either don't drive or don't want to pay exorbitant parking fees downtown or don't want to drive around the French Quarter for two hours on a Sunday afternoon looking for a parking space bigger than a dirt bike. The streetcar is also a lifeline for those who stayed at Fat Harry's a few hours longer than intended and are too drunk to drive home and don't have enough money left for a taxi.

Just off the streetcar line in either direction are some of the most unique and (sometimes) wonderful neighborhoods in the city, populated with a collection of the world's most unique people, an eclectic gumbo of nuts, weirdoes, mild (and not-so-mild) eccentrics; gay and straight (and a few undecided); male, female and those of confused gender; Catholics, Jews, Buddhists, new agers and necromancers; some bright lights, some dim bulbs; rich, poor, middle-class, destitute; the upright, the downfallen, the uptight, the flexible; the never sober, the sometimes sober, the abstainers; the young pierced and tattooed standing at the streetcar stop next to little old ladies with bright red hair still carrying old Maison Blanche bags; Africans, Europeans, Asians, Native Americans, Latin Americans, East Indians, Middle Easterners, and more than a handful of interplanetary travelers waiting for the mothership to take them home — you name it, we've got it, they all live here.

For those of you reading this book whom are among the unfortunate souls who have never lived in or spent much, if any, time in the wonderful Crescent City, I am genuinely sorry. New Orleans is a unique experience — there is no other place in the world like it. I have tried to paint an accurate picture of an uptown New Orleans neighborhood with all its glorious occupants, but to truly understand our culture, you must come here and mingle among us, if you are brave enough.

A local coffee commercial came out a few years ago that said it all. To paraphrase: Every year millions of people come down here to sample our wonderful food, listen to our music, and try to dance like we do. But you're already here. Count your blessings.

Margrete Grey Wolf
New Orleans, LA
May 2005

JUST OFF THE STREETCAR LINE
(a New Orleans melodrama)

"Southern Louisiana isn't really a part of the United States, you know, it's actually Northern Jamaica." (Overheard at Civil District Court, Parish of Orleans).

Lucille Fontenot watched old Mr. Charley Byrd rummage through his neighbors' curbside trash cans with a flashlight, something he did two mornings a week from three o'clock until approximately four-thirty, up and down the block. He had been raiding the trash for the past eleven years, ever since he retired from the New Orleans Police Department. He was now seventy-six and his nocturnal habit seemed to be one of his few sources of entertainment. His wife, Geneva, had left him twelve years ago to marry a used car salesman from Picayune, Mississippi, and he had gotten progressively weirder ever since. Lucille didn't know if Mr. Charley had any other hobbies. He rarely came outside before late afternoon and he wasn't exactly sociable.

When Lucille first discovered Mr. Charley going through her garbage, she stepped out on the porch and asked him what the Sam Hill he was doing, messing around in other people's trash. He just glared at her and told her to stop interfering with important business. The next day she called the police and reported him, but they told her unless he left a mess, there was no law against going through people's trash if he wasn't actually standing on their property. She had watched nightly after that, trying to catch him standing in her little front yard, but he always stood on the sidewalk or the street to do his rummaging, so she gave up. When she told her best friend next door, Leola Broussard, about Mr. Charley's nightly raids, they agreed they should burn all their important trash. At first they tried burning it in the toilet, but when they melted Lucille's toilet seat while burning old car insurance papers, they decided to use the kitchen sink instead. After they caught Lucille's kitchen curtains on fire disposing of bank statements going back five years, they gave up on barbecuing their trash.

Lucille would probably have never noticed Mr. Charley's nighttime activities if her husband hadn't died about the same time Charley Byrd started trash diving. After Freddie passed away, Lucille developed insomnia, so she was up most of the night, wandering around in her pink chenille bathrobe, drinking Barq's rootbeer for her indigestion and reading murder mysteries until she finally nodded off about four o'clock. This morning was no different. After watching Mr. Charley for about twenty minutes, Lucille finished her Barq's and settled in bed with a book called *The Muff Murders*, a mystery novel about a fat prostitute who murdered men by sitting on their faces until they expired. She finally fell asleep a little after four.

Lucille awoke at ten-thirty, fed her big white cat, Telemachus, and took a bath. After dusting herself liberally with gardenia talcum powder, she pulled on a neon green shorts set she'd bought when Woolworth's went out of business on Canal Street. Leola called it "baby-shit green" but she didn't care; Lucille liked bright colors. She then opened up all her windows, put the coffee on, and heated up the red beans and rice from last night's dinner. She was just pouring boiled milk into the pot of chicory coffee when Leola tapped on the back screen door and let herself in. "I brought you some okra," she said, dropping a plastic bag on the counter. "I can't eat this slimy stuff. Reminds me of garden slugs."

Lucille stirred the red beans on the stove. "Then why do you grow it?"

"My mama grew it. Besides, you eat it."

As Leola went through her usual ritual of adding steamed milk, Steen's cane syrup and nutmeg to her coffee, Lucille ladled beans and rice into two bowls and set them on the table. Leola was dousing her beans with tobasco when she suddenly looked up and stared at her friend's head. "Girl, what color did you use on your hair this time?"

Lucille patted her locks. "The box said 'Evening Primrose'."

Leola snorted. "Looks more like K&B purple to me."

"I like it. Besides, it'll wash out in three weeks. Next month I'll be another color."

"Why don't you just go gray?"

Lucille stared at her friend's dyed blonde locks but thought better of mentioning her own romance with peroxide. She tore off a hunk of French bread and said, "I'll never go gray. That's why God made Miss Clairol. Gray hair just makes you look old."

"We are old."

"Speak for yourself. I'm not ready for Depends yet."

Leola crossed herself. "God help us. If I ever get to that point, just shoot me and bury me out in the back yard. And don't you dare let my sister come to my funeral."

"Leola, I can't stop Evelina from coming to your funeral!"

"Yes you can, it's in my will. And soon's I'm dead, you call the Salvation Army and tell them to come take everything outta my house except the stuff you want and what I left to my kids. That bitch isn't going to get so much as one place setting out of my china cabinet. That's in the will, too."

"Do ya'll even remember why you're not speaking?"

"Of course I remember! Before Mama died, she promised me her entire Elvis collection. Then before she could make out a will, she ups and chokes on a barbecued shrimp and falls face first into a big bowl of dirty rice and expires. Her body was still warm when Evelina went over there and cleaned out everything in the collection. By the time I got to the house, there wasn't so much as a rhinestone left. So don't you let that little sneak come to my funeral. The only reason she'd come anyway is to snicker at me one last time."

Lucille took the bowls to the sink and filled them with water. "What if I kick the bucket first?"

"I never thought about that. I just always assumed I'd go first. Maybe 'cause I can't imagine living without you right here next door."

Lucille took a pitcher of iced tea out of the refrigerator and set it on the table. "You never know when it's your time, Leola. Look what happened to my Freddie. Fifty-two years old and he drops dead from the chicken attack."

"But that was an accident. It wasn't like he had a disease or something."

Lucille poured tea into purple Krewe of Bacchus plastic tumblers. "You know, I always thought he'd be eaten by an alligator or attacked by a nutria, something like that. I mean, anybody who becomes a surveyor in southeast Louisiana is just plain thick. All you do is stand around in the swamps up to your chest in gunk, or run around in the woods out in New Orleans East, dodging snakes and wild pigs and criminals. I don't know which is worse, the water moccasins or the rejects from the projects."

Leola grunted. "I'd rather be stuck down in Cocodrie at midnight without bug spray than walk through the projects with Jesus on a Sunday morning."

"That's pretty much what Freddie said. At least in the swamps you have a chance of survival. But after all those years out there in the marsh, the only things that ever bit him were the mosquitoes, and then he goes and gets killed by an attack chicken."

"Technically, it wasn't the chicken that killed him."

Lucille lifted a big pan of blackberry cobbler from the top of the stove and spooned generous helpings into two bowls. "No, *technically* he died of a heart attack, but it was the chicken that *gave* him the heart attack when it flew at Freddie outta nowhere, squawking and landing on his head, pecking at him. Turned out to be that bayou bozo's attack chicken. I mean, I've heard of junkyard pigs and guard alligators, but never in my life had I ever heard of an attack chicken." She added vanilla ice cream to the cobbler.

"Well, at least Freddie's partner shot the stupid chicken."

"Lotta good it did my Freddie. And then the dumb coonass who owned the chicken tried to sue the government for a hundred thousand dollars for the loss of that psychotic chicken!"

"At least Freddie's death was ruled job related and you got a good widow's pension."

"Yeah, but it didn't bring my Freddie back. I haven't eaten chicken since that very day." They picked up their drinks and cobbler and headed through the shotgun house to the second parlor. It was time for "All My Children".

*****

Charley Byrd sat in his red and white kitchen in his underwear, eating a fried egg sandwich and drinking industrial strength Community coffee, listening to his police scanner. There was a B & E in progress on Fig Street, a corner grocery had just been held up in Gert Town, there had been a shooting at a bar on lower Magazine Street, and a six-year old and his mother were in custody for starting a fight on the Carrollton bus and throwing eggs at another passenger. The usual stuff, nothing to threaten his neighborhood. Some days were more exciting than others. One day last week an alligator had been discovered swimming in a pool behind a house on Octavia Street; the owner was found crouching in a mimosa tree, naked as a jaybird, screaming her head off. And yesterday some little crackhead had tried to rob a three hundred fifty pound transvestite named Rhonda on Dumaine Street. He/she knocked down the little twerp and sat on him until a cop showed up. The perpetrator put up a fight, however, and in the process, Rhonda's red wig was destroyed and one of his/her falsies was punctured.

Mr. Charley finished his meal, placed his dishes in the sink, and quietly walked through the little shotgun house to the front room, taking his police scanner with him. The only light in the house was either electric or came from the transoms over the doors, twelve feet up. The window shades were taped to the sills and window frames with duct tape, and navy blue sheets were hung over all the windows except the bathroom. Charley had cut little slits in the shades, though, so he could spy on his neighbors. Burglar bars protected all the windows, but that's a common sight in New Orleans.

When Geneva Byrd left twelve years ago, she had taken absolutely every household item with her including the nails that held up the pictures on the walls. When Charley returned from a bass fishing rodeo in Florida, he found nothing but his clothes in the closet and his shaving kit in the bathroom. Geneva had even taken the used soap in the bathroom, the nails out of the walls and the ice cube trays out of the freezer. Since then he had furnished his home with ugly, utilitarian furniture from thrift stores and the trash. The house was completely devoid of photographs, art work, knick-knacks or anything personal except the stacks of books and magazines lined up on the floor against the wall. Nine years before his wife's departure, his daughter Eileen, who hated both her parents with a royal passion, had gotten up one Saturday morning, loaded up her Ford Mustang, and driven off without so much as a kiss-my-ass, never to be heard from again. It was the day after her high school graduation. Being a cop at the time, Mr. Charley had discovered six months later that Eileen had obtained a driver's license from the state of Florida and was working as a stripper at a club called Hit 'n' Run near Ft. Lauderdale. Upon discovery that his only child was pole dancing naked in South Florida, Mr. Charley just sighed and regretted that he'd never really gotten to know his pretty blonde daughter. He never regretted losing his wife, nor did he wonder where she'd gone; he knew very well that the former Mrs. Byrd had moved to Picayune with the guy who sold him his truck as soon as the ink was dry on the divorce papers. Charley held no grudge against the poor SOB, though. On the contrary, he wished the old bastard luck—Geneva was a pain in the ass.

Mr. Charley settled into his cracked and duct-taped recliner to read the paper. He paid particular attention to stories about the latest airplane crash, the imminent indictment of a former governor of Louisiana, and the presidential sex scandal. Even though there was a great deal of evidence to the contrary, he decided that Puerto Rican terrorists had blown up the plane, the FBI was picking on the ex-governor because they hated Cajuns, and the President's ex-girlfriend was really Castro's mistress, sent to spy on the United States. And somehow or other it was all tied together in one big plot to overthrow the U.S. government. Not that he was *against* overthrowing the U.S. government. Mr. Charley belonged to a group that called themselves Sons of the South, which advocated Louisiana's secession from the Union. Currently, there were only four members, all of them disgruntled old white men from uptown New Orleans, but they were hoping to attract more members in the near future. They had no idea how to go about seceding, having used an old copy of *Gone With the Wind* as their only reference book, and their meetings had produced exactly one piece of paper, a rambling manifesto that was nothing more than a tirade against Yankees, the National Organization for Women, Vietnamese refugees, the IRS, Jesse Jackson, Michael Jackson, Harvard University, the current Mayor of New Orleans, Jamaicans, Japanese cars, Mexican beer and Chihuahuas. (They had voted against adding tacos, Chinese food and Nicaraguans to the list since they were all frequent diners at Taco Bell and Ding's Dragon Den, and one of the members of the group was married to a Nicaraguan woman.) Actually, their weekly meetings consisted mainly of playing poker, smoking cheap cigars and griping about life in general. They all agreed that the quality of life in New Orleans began to deteriorate about the time the Interstate was built in the mid-1960's. It was all downhill from there.

Mr. Charley flipped through a copy of *Field & Stream*, watched a rerun of *Gilligan's Island*, yelled at Oprah for twenty minutes, then fell asleep during the second episode of a *Mister Ed* marathon. He always took a nap in the afternoon so he'd be fresh and alert for his evening activities.

*****

Just Off the Streetcar Line

Dave Richard adjusted his silver tie in the mirror, ran a comb through his silver hair, and grabbed his pale gray suit jacket from the back of the desk chair in his bedroom. Dave was a snappy dresser, and he liked being color coordinated. He was a nice looking man who turned a lot of heads, but mainly because he looked enough like Governor Edwards to cause ten double-takes a day.

Dave's remarkable resemblance to the infamous ex-governor had its pluses. He had once posed for pictures with two bubbly female college students from the University of Alabama who gave him a kiss and asked if they could call him Edwin. He said, "Oh what the hell, just call me Eddie." And there were the occasional requests for autographs and changes in the legislature. But the most bizarre incident had occurred at a bar on Magazine Street.

Dave had wandered into a little neighborhood bar late one Friday afternoon and was enjoying a big frosty mug of Corona when a very busty, very drunk young lady sitting on a barstool next to him offered to service him in the backseat of his limo all the way back to Baton Rouge. She said he was the cutest governor Louisiana had ever produced and she wanted to show her support. As Dave was reflecting that her boobs could probably support quintuplets, the young lady unzipped Dave's pants and offered to give him a sneak preview. Dave jumped off the barstool and told her if she rode with him to Baton Rouge he would have to share her with his bodyguard. Her response was, "Is he as cute as you?" When Dave pointed out the biggest, ugliest, drunkest gorilla in the bar and told her that he was Dave's head of security, "King Kong Bergeron", Miss Big Tits withdrew her offer and turned her attentions to a good looking black guy in a baseball cap sitting on the other side of Dave. Mr. Baseball Cap told her his name was Sammy Sosa and she could ride in the back of his limo any time.

Dave finished his beer without incident and was headed for the door when, on a whim, he made the mistake of approaching his "head of security". He clapped the big gorilla on the back and said, "Thanks for being there for me, man." The gorilla, who was trying desperately to light a cigarette but couldn't connect cigarette with lighter, squinted up at Dave and said, "Any time, Governor." At that moment Dave noticed that the gorilla was sporting a live green garden lizard wearing a little string leash around its neck. The lizard would dart in and out of King Kong's shirt pocket, occasionally hanging from the big ape's extremely hairy chest. When Dave remarked on the unusual pet, Kong said, "That's Tarzan, man, he lives in my shirt pocket." Tarzan, being a creature of sound mind, ducked into Kong's pocket just as the lighter flame connected with Kong's long, dirty hair. In a panic, Dave threw a glass of beer on the small brush fire, staring in horror at the dripping, singed, incredibly ugly hulk now standing before him like Swamp Thing. Just as Dave feared for life and limb, the hulk grabbed him in a bear hug and slurred, "You saved my life, man. I'm your friend forever!" This maneuver brought Dave eyeball-to-eyeball with Tarzan, who had crawled out to survey the damage. Tarzan freaked out and jumped on Dave's nose, clinging for dear life to the slippery surface. Dave squeaked out "lizard!" and Kong loosened his grip on Dave, pulling the lizard off Dave's face as he fell back onto the barstool. "Looka that! He loves ya' man!" Dave decided it was time to exit the building before the lizard attacked any more of his body parts. Besides, he now smelled like a drunk chimpanzee.

Dave's wife Judy wandered into the bedroom and looked at her husband's reflection in the dresser mirror. "I liked the pink tie better."

Dave shook his head. "Made me look like a flamer."

Judy patted him on the ass and said that could be a real plus in certain circumstances. Dave replied that since his client this morning was an ex-football player nicknamed "Boxcar", he thought he should dress more like George Hamilton than Liberace. Of course, you could never tell. He had once sold a condo in the Warehouse District to a hockey player who shown up at the door of his French Quarter apartment in full make-up, a white feather boa, a pink kimono and neon green rollerblades, and he was carrying a little poodle whose fur was dyed a revolting shade of magenta. Dave couldn't have cared less about the hockey player's attire, but the goddamned dog yipped and yapped the whole time, then threw its little pink body at Dave's leg and tried to fuck his ankle. That was when Dave lost his cool and called the little varmint a reindeer cunt and flipped it across the courtyard into the goldfish pond. He was surprised that he didn't lose the sale. The hockey player just fished the bedraggled little ankle-humper out of the pond, wrapped it up in a pink towel and said, "Now that's what you get for messing with strange men. It lands you in a world of shit every time." Dave, who was silently grateful that he wasn't strangled with the feather boa, apologized for losing his cool, but the hockey player just shrugged and said, "Oh it happens all the time; she's an obnoxious little tramp."

Dave loved his work. He sold residential real estate, and he was very good at it, partly due to his passion for the beautiful old homes in New Orleans and his knowledge of their architecture and history, but mostly because Dave was a born salesman. His best friend Willie had once remarked that Dave Richard could sell the spokes off a bicycle to a ten-year-old kid. Dave had consequently built up a very successful real estate agency in uptown New Orleans and, at age fifty-one, had made enough money to buy a mansion in the Garden District and retire. The thought of moving out of the neighborhood of his birth again, however, left him cold; he had tried it a couple of times, with disappointing results, and he had finally moved back into his family home when his father died thirteen years earlier. He had first tried living closer to the Loyola campus during his college years, but found himself at his mother's dining room table at least three nights a week, so after his first year of college he had moved into his parents' carriage house in the back of their main house. After he and Judy married, they lived in the neighborhood until sixteen years ago, when they decided to buy a house in Old Metairie. It was the first time either of them had ever lived outside Orleans Parish and the experience left them feeling lonely and out of their element. Three years later when Dave's father died, Dave's mother asked him if he wanted to buy the house from her. She wanted to downsize and live in the carriage house with her two cats, Heckel and Jeckel; that big old barn was just too much for her now, but she didn't want to sell to strangers and live somewhere else, either. So Dave and Judy happily moved back to New Orleans with their son Clifton, who was now twenty-three and in his second year of law school at NYU. Unlike his parents, he couldn't wait to get out of New Orleans and live in a completely different environment. Clifton was currently sharing an apartment in Greenwich Village with a sweet little girl named Heather, whom Dave sincerely hoped Clifton had the good sense to marry. Men needed good wives to keep them sane. As Dave watched Judy rummage through her closet, he silently thanked God again for bringing this smart, good looking woman into his life twenty-six years ago.

Judy Sauvage Richard was not only smart and still very good looking at age fifty, she was also a successful interior decorator for the simple reason that she always gave the customer what he or she really wanted. If a man wanted a pool table in the middle of his dining room and a motorcycle resting on the living room floor in front of his fifty-five inch TV, a

Barbarella poster set inside a $5,500 antique French gold frame, and a purple crushed velvet pit group surrounding a faux zebra rug, far be it for Judy to tell him his house looked like Graceland. And if a woman asked for a red ceiling, green velvet drapes and carved Victorian over-stuffed chairs and sofas upholstered in rose-patterned damask, Judy did not tell her client that her living room looked like Christmas on an acid trip, she gave Mrs. Nouveau-Riche-with-No-Taste exactly what she wanted, a red and green nightmare. When Judy's sister Charlotte asked her how she could stand to decorate for such troglodytes, Judy said, "It doesn't bother me at all; I don't have to live there."

Judy's favorite clients were the ones who appreciated fine antiques, hardwood floors and oriental rugs, plenty of light, paintings that somewhat resembled their subject matter, and a minimum of knick-knacks. And the bulk of her clients fell into that general category, but there were still a few of the troglodyte variety. However, every client happily paid the bill because Judy provided what they asked for, regardless of her opinion of their taste, which was why Judy's client this morning, Joey Comeaux, was thrilled with the work she had done on his property.

Joey had gotten rich beyond his wildest dreams in the waste disposal business, and a few months earlier he decided to spend some of his hard earned money decorating his fishing camp to resemble Cleopatra's barge. So Judy had set about making Joey's camp at Lake Maurepas look like the Queen of the Nile's

Just Off the Streetcar Line

bedroom, which required yards and yards of silk draping old cypress walls and grass mats covering the weatherboard floors. Joey insisted on spray painting the grass mats metallic gold and scattering cheesy, fake Egyptian statuettes all over the big room, so that was exactly what Judy gave him. She also bought a camel saddle from Pier One, an exotic old iron bed with mosquito netting from a flea market, and hired a belly dancer to come out once a week and dance for Joey because he expressed a desire for "one a' them harem girls in a pink genie suit" to dance for him (Joey was a big "I Dream of Jeannie" fan). Judy was meeting with Joey this morning to discuss their next foray into the decorating world, Joey's hunting camp near Franklinton, which he wanted to look "just like the Ponderosa." She selected old, soft blue jeans, a plaid shirt and comfortable walking shoes for the ride up to the woods north of the lake. It was going to be a long day.

Dave's day promised to be more urban and less exotic. Boxcar's current home, which he wanted to sell, was located near Children's Hospital, so today Dave was visiting the site to take photographs and meet the client in person for the first time. Boxcar wanted to buy a bigger house in the uptown area, and Dave had several listings in mind for him. He knew he would find just the right home for his client.

Dave was an incurable optimist, a happy person who looked forward to each new day as an adventure. He walked out of his front door whistling the theme song from the Jolly Green Giant commercials, threw his briefcase on the front seat of his silver BMW, and backed carefully out of his narrow driveway, ready to meet the world.

*****

Jackie Cheramie let herself into her empty house, locked the door behind her, dumped her backpack in a chair, then stripped off her school uniform and threw it on the floor, kicking it ferociously. "Soon as I graduate, I'm gonna burn that fucking uniform," she muttered, heading for the bathroom. She slipped out of her jungle print underwear, scrutinized her beautiful eighteen-year-old body in the full-length mirror, and stepped into the shower to wash off another unsatisfactory day at Our Lady of Shining Light High School.

Jackie finished her shower then wandered around in the nude, picking up her things and once again admiring her mother's new purple sofa. She had to admit, Lisa had great taste. She might be a space cadet, but she sure knew how to decorate. Their bungalow style home was a clever mixture of art deco, Victorian, southwestern, oriental, modern and traditional. Jackie called it "early wacko", but it worked. It was a perfect reflection of Lisa's personality.

Jackie walked around the house in complete comfort; she was alone for a few days. She wasn't expecting anyone to knock on the door, Grandmama was dead, and Lisa was in Las Vegas with some guy named Frank. Jackie sincerely hoped her mother's latest romance worked out, but she wasn't holding her breath. When it came to men, Lisa's brain was buried somewhere in the back yard. In fact, Jackie knew her mother's elevator didn't make it to the top floors on a good day, but she loved Lisa and endeavored to take care of her. She knew she could never let her mother live alone.

Jackie considered herself extremely lucky in life. She knew damned well if Grandmama Theriot hadn't left them this house and all that money, she and her mother would be working at McDonald's and living in a two-room apartment on Felicity Street. Or worse. That is, if her mother could *handle* a job at McDonald's. Jackie had her doubts. Her mother had never actually *worked* in her whole life, although lately she had sold quite a few of her paintings. Jackie thought her mother's artwork was God-awful, but people seemed to like ugly paintings of popeyed green cats and emaciated pink dogs. Lisa had definitely done too much acid in the early seventies. Jackie had no idea how she herself had turned out so normal, considering her genetic background.

Jackie's father, Leon Cheramie, was an alcoholic tugboat captain her mother had married when she was nineteen and divorced two years later, right after Jackie was born. Just as well; Leon's family was a mangy bunch of fishermen, trappers and drunks from lower Plaquemines Parish. Jackie really didn't remember him at all. When she was two years old, her father got drunk one night and fell into the Mississippi River. His body was found three days later, about four miles downstream, wedged in between some pilings, being slowly consumed by wildlife. Since Leon's death, Lisa had had three rather brief marriages: one to an artist who was more interested in sniffing glue than painting; one to a Mexican waiter who was angling for a green card (and who neglected to mention his wife and four children in Vera Cruz); and the last to a high school football coach who had a very unfamilial interest in his fifteen-year-old step-daughter. He departed one rainy evening when Jackie threatened to give him a circumcision with an exacto knife.

Jackie pulled on a long red Mickey Mouse tee-shirt, put on a Lisa Loeb CD and settled into a big overstuffed chair with *White Oleanders*. Her best friend Annie Gaudet said she didn't see how Jackie could read that kind of heavy-duty stuff, but then Annie considered a Danielle Steele novel heavy reading.

Jackie wasn't sure why Annie was her best friend, because intellectually they were like night and day. But they'd been inseparable since kindergarten. They would have to separate somewhat next fall, though, because Jackie already had a full scholarship to Tulane University, and Annie — well, she wasn't sure what was going to happen to Annie. Jackie hoped her best friend wouldn't wind up dancing naked in the Quarter, like her mother had. Francine Gaudet's specialty had been to dangle live crawfish from her nipples and make them dance. She had demonstrated this fine art to Jackie and Annie at last year's Fourth of July crawfish boil, a feat that had inspired Annie to consider a career in exotic dancing. Lately Jackie had been trying to talk her friend into going to John Jay's to learn how to cut hair.

When the phone rang, Jackie looked at the caller ID and sighed. Michael. She picked up the phone and purred, "Hello, gorgeous."

"Hello, sweet thing. Are you alone?"

"All alone and nobody to play with."

"Where's Lisa?"

"She's in Las Vegas with l'homme du jour."

Michael breathed into the phone. "I could come over."

"You could. I'm not wearing any underwear."

Michael's breathing got heavier. "I can be there in fifteen minutes."

"I'll be waiting."

Jackie hung up and sighed again. She really needed to do something about Michael, but she just wasn't ready to give him up yet. He was sweet and kind and a great lay, and he'd be a wonderful boyfriend except for that pesky little matter of his cute little wife.

*****

Anthony Guidry was sitting on his bedroom floor trying to repair a hole in his blow-up doll with a bicycle patch. He carefully glued the little square to Giselle's thigh, then tenderly placed her between his mattress and box springs. Giselle had been the name on the box she came in, and he'd been calling her that ever since. He was currently between girlfriends, so Giselle came in handy every now and then. It was hard to find a girlfriend when you were twenty-seven years old, worked part-time at night, attended school four days a week, and lived with your mother. Especially *his* mother.

Sharp raps on his bedroom door interrupted his tranquility. "Ant'ny! Dinnuh's ready! Come on, dah'lin, don't let the grease set on them chicken laigs, you wanna eat 'em while they hot. An' I got some crabs your Uncle Lou brought up from the bayou last Sat'dy, remember he was over for lunch? They been sittin' in the icebox all this time; I had to cook 'em or they wouldda gone bad. An' I got some fresh beans and tomatoes from my cousin Gina's garden and cream potatoes. I been cookin' all afternoon. I even got some bread pudding sittin' on the counter, but it's still too hot to eat, you gotta let it set a little bit. You got to save some, though, I'm takin' a bowl by my sistah's house later. She never could learn to cook bread pudding. Always burns it." She stopped momentarily to suck in air. "Ant'ny! You dead in there?" The nasal Chalmatian tones seeped through the cracks of the door and filled the room like a noxious gas. Anyone living outside of southeast Louisiana would have placed Rosemarie Guidry's accent right smack in the middle of Brooklyn, but anyone from New Orleans would have immediately known where she was born and raised. There is no other sound in the world like the voice of a middle-aged Chalmette housewife.

Anthony immediately smoothed his plaid bedspread and kicked his dirty clothes under the bed. "No, ma, I ain't dead. I'll be right out."

"Well you hurry up, you gotta be at work for six. Sav-a-Center won't wait for you forever."

Anthony opened up his door and stared at his mother. Two hundred eighty pounds and growing, he thought to himself. "Ma, it's only four-fifteen. I got plenty of time."

"I know, baby, but you shouldn't bolt your food like no deckhand. You'll get gas."

Anthony headed for the dining room, where there was enough food laid out to feed a family of six. "Ma, you got three places set. Somebody else coming to dinner?"

Mrs. Guidry sat down and poured herself a glass of iced tea. "Tammy's comin' over, she'll be here in a little while." Anthony groaned and started piling his plate with food. "You be nice to her, she's your baby sistah. She's depressed. She just left that bum Jerry."

Anthony muttered "another one bites the dust" while devouring a chicken leg. "Don't talk with ya' mouth full. I just thank the lawd she nevuh married that little bastid. He's gonna wind up in prison, mark my word."

"If he keeps stealing cars, yeah, I guess so!" Anthony shook his head. "Boy, Tammy sure can pick 'em."

"Oh, she ain't done so bad."

"Are you kiddin' me, Ma? First she runs off with that moron from the gas station when she's sixteen, stays gone two months, then she comes back and cries for a couple weeks. So then she goes and shacks up with numb-nuts Nathan, who has the IQ of a freeze-dried wart and a personality to match. And then when she dumped *him*, she took up with that idiot Marvin who thought he was a werewolf and went around growling at people on the full moon and jumping at 'em from the bushes."

His mother shook her head. "Marvin was harmless, poor baby, he just wanted some attention. Poor little Marvin, his mothuh nevuh loved him, left him all the time with her sistah who worked the snowball stand at City Park. Marvin just rode the rides all day and ate junk food. Curdled his stomach."

"Curdled his brain, was more like it." Anthony shoveled in mashed potatoes. "Well, Marvin may have been harmless, but Lester wasn't."

Just Off the Streetcar Line

Mrs. Guidry's face darkened. "He ever comes around here again, I'll kill his skinny little ass." Just sit on him, Anthony thought, that'll kill the little fart.

"I don't think he's ever coming back over here, Ma, not after you steamed his balls with an iron."

"Now you know that was an accident. I was aimin' to hit him in the head with the iron and then he tripped over the chair and I hit the steam button by accident and cooked his little weenie. He deserved it. Nobody's gonna get drunk and hit *my* baby."

Anthony grabbed another chicken leg. "You'd think after the Lester disaster Tammy would've learned to be a little choosier."

"You ain't had such good luck with the girls, Mr. Prince Chaumin'. You been kicked out by three women in the last two and a half years. You doin' somethin' wrong."

"Yeah, I'm picking the wrong women, that's what I'm doing wrong."

His mother snorted at him. "Maybe if you'd pick a girl whose brain is bigger than her boobs you'd have better luck."

Anthony could think of no suitable reply, so he finished his meal in silence while his mother ran her mouth. When she finally got up to retrieve the bread pudding from the kitchen, Anthony breathed a sigh of relief. "I gotta get my own apartment," he mumbled. He ate a bowl of bread pudding, told his mother it was a good dinner, then grabbed his car keys and sprinted out of the house before he had a chance of running into his sister. Seven hours at the grocery store would be absolute heaven after listening to his mother for the last forty-five minutes.

As soon as she saw her son's Trans Am roar off down the street, Rosemarie got up from the table and lumbered into Anthony's room. She pulled the dirty clothes out from under the bed, snooped through his closet and dresser drawers, then pulled up the mattress and looked at Giselle. Rosemarie shook her head, dropped the mattress and exited the room. "Ant'ny," she muttered, "you gotta get a life, baby."

*****

Miss Buelah Mae Johnson stood at her front window and watched Anthony tear down the street. "Uh-uh. Dat boy gonna wreck dat hot rod o' his, he don't be more careful drivin' dat thing. Thinks dis here's da Indanap'lis Five Hunnert." Miss Buelah went back to hanging chicken feet from her curtain rod. Her ten-year-old granddaughter Clarice stood behind her and watched in fascination.

"Big Mama, why you hangin' dead chicken parts from the curtain rod?"

Miss Buelah ambled into the dining room and suspended a dried frog from the window shade pull. "Dey be good medicine, baby. Keep da devils out."

Clarice followed her grandmother into the dining room and swung from the fireplace mantle. "What's the frog for?"

"Brings da rain, chile, brings da rain. Been awful dry aroun' here lately."

They made their way through the bedrooms, where Miss Buelah sprinkled dried rose petals and rosemary on the beds ("to bring sweet dreams an' keep a good man in yo' bed"), then finally into the kitchen, where she hung up a small mojo bag filled with corn meal, red beans, a little rice, a wishbone and some filé powder ("so we don't never go hongry"). Her mission accomplished, she turned toward the chicken frying on the stove. "Gonna be a good supper, tonight, baby, got some fried chicken and mustard greens and got me a big ole pot a' black eyed peas. Got a skillet a' cornbread over here, too. Git me some butter out the icebox, baby girl."

Clarice retrieved the butter from the ancient Fridgidaire and set it on the counter. "What's in the oven, Big Mama?"

"Choc'lit cake, honey. Yo' Uncle Leroy's comin' home from da' jailhouse today, praise da lawd. He done paid his debt to society."

"Why's he been in jail?"

"Yo' uncle got in wif a bad crowd."

Clarice lifted up the lid to inspect the pot of black-eyed peas. "What'd they do?"

Her grandmother sighed and turned over the chicken. "Dey got drunk and stole a animal control truck from da pound. Den dey went over by City Park and catched a buncha ducks in a fishin' net and took 'em over to one a' dem big buildings downtown and dumped 'em in da fountain. Dey was ducks and feathers and duck doody *ever*'where! Da judge give 'em all ninety days for public drunkenness, takin' wild animals outta der habitat, and makin' a big mess. Dey didn't git in no trouble for da truck 'cause da pound say it weren't ders. Turned out it was a truck from up at Bogalusa, but nobody knows how it got down here." She turned to glare at Clarice. "Don't never drink no alkihol, baby girl, dey's a devil in ever' bottle, and yo' uncle's da livin' proof!"

"I won't never drink that stuff, Big Mama."

Miss Buelah gave her granddaughter a hug. "You my precious baby. Here, stir dis here pot while I set da table."

*****

Louie Bourgeois was watching Mrs. Johnson hang chicken feet in her front window when he heard furtive tapping at his side door. Lilly Hebert was standing on the stoop, nervously biting her nails and glancing around her. His clients generally slipped down the alleyway to his side door and stood in the recess where they wouldn't be seen from the street. (He never understood why; people in New Orleans eventually find out everything about everybody. Few secrets in that fair city are kept for very long.)

For some reason people tended to confuse private detectives with the Secret Service or the CIA. Louie knew investigators who took themselves seriously, bought into what he referred to as the "Batman Bullshit Syndrome". But Louie had a sense of humor. Although his business was named Bourgeois Investigations, on the very bottom of his business cards, in tiny print, were the words "Secret Squirrel, P.I."

Louie locked the door behind Lilly and took her to his office in the back of the house. She sat on the edge of the red leather chair (a nod to Nero Wolf), clutching her purse. "I came as soon as I got your call."

Louie settled into the green swivel chair behind the scarred mahogany desk that had sat in his father's law office for forty years. Louie wasn't sentimental, he just couldn't see putting out several hundred dollars on a new desk when he had a perfectly good one at his disposal. The rest of his house mirrored his bachelor attitude, for although Louie rarely went for long without female companionship, it was very obvious that he lived alone. His house was decorated in what one girlfriend had dubbed "early Swahili". His living room decor actually included two beanbag chairs, a lava lamp and a velvet painting of a bullfighter. His "draperies" were shower curtains from Wal-Mart. A poker table sat in the kitchen, and his bedroom was adorned with posters of *Playboy* centerfolds. There were no wreaths or flower arrangements, no French watercolors, no chintz draperies, Oriental rugs or delicate Queen Anne furniture, and there was certainly no china, crystal, silver or table linen. For that matter, there was no dining room furniture—a full-sized pool table filled up the entire dining room. He had been married once long ago for six months and six days. It was a failed experiment. His lovely young bride soon declared him a hopeless Neanderthal and departed in a cloud of Chanel No. 5. Two years later she married a doctor, bought a half-million dollar house and became an interior decorator. Louie stayed single, lived off pizzas and microwavable dinners, and dated a lot of waitresses.

Louie inherited his lack of decorating skills from his mother. Vivienne Bourgeouis came from a prominent New Orleans family and had grown up in a beautiful old mansion filled with Queen Anne and Duncan Fyffe antiques, Persian rugs, damask draperies, and Ming vases. Her own home, however, looked like a cross between the set of *Auntie Mame* and a Turkish bazaar, with a hint of voodoo and *The Addams Family* thrown in to make things interesting. Louie figured his current home was a reflection of his formative years. The truth, of course, was that Louie never grew up. He wasn't cheap, he just didn't see any reason to change; hence the college dorm décor.

Just Off the Streetcar Line

Louie sat and looked at Lilly, wondering what her reaction would be when he showed her the photographs of her husband in certain compromising positions with his secretary, wearing nothing but golf cleats and an LSU Tigers football helmet. Louie had learned over the years never to second-guess a woman's reaction to graphic evidence of her husband's indiscretions. Some laughed, some cried, most got angry once the shock wore off. One gorgeous blonde client with legs up to her neck taped all the pictures of her husband to the wall in Louie's office, then took a revolver out of her purse and shot the genitals out of every photo. She handed Louie a check for his services, plus damages to the wall, told him to mail the pictures to her husband signed "Love and Kisses, Lorraine," then declared that she was headed to the bank to clean out all their accounts. Most clients were not so dramatic, however. He was pretty sure Lilly was a weeper.

Louie slowly removed the photos of Mr. Hebert from the envelope and handed them to Lilly who, as predicted, dissolved into a puddle in the chair. He gave her a box of tissues and a shot of brandy, then handed her the business card of Lamont T. Verges, Attorney at Law. There was nothing more he could do other than wish her a successful divorce.

After Lilly left, Louie called another client with the happy news that he had pictures she could use in court. This case was a little stickier than some, and Louie thought it might be a good idea to get Mrs. Menendez a little drunk before he gave her the photos, since they showed Mr. Menendez performing crimes against nature with a male prostitute and a St. Bernard. Louie looked at the pictures and sighed. Nothing much had changed in his twenty years as a private detective — some people just couldn't keep their zippers up or their underwear on — but the population seemed to have gotten sicker the last five years or so. As Louie flipped through the snapshots, he came across a particularly engaging image of Mr. Menendez crawling around on all fours, wearing a spiked dog collar and being spanked with a leash. He set a bottle of brandy and two glasses on his desk and sat back to wait for Mrs. Menendez. It wouldn't take her long to get there; she just lived five blocks away.

*****

Mrs. Eugenia Robichaux sat in her kitchen shelling butterbeans and crowder peas, bounty from the vegetable garden that completely covered her backyard. She had beans growing up the side fence, squash hanging from the back fence, merlitons dangling from the clotheslines, a grape arbor sheltering what had once been a barbecue pit but now served as an herb garden. Tomato cages lined the sunny side of the house, beans climbed up the skeleton of an old swing set, and every inch of what had been open yard at some point was filled with pepper bushes, broccoli, mustard greens, peas, okra. A fig tree stood at one end of the yard, and a pecan tree shaded the house on the opposite corner; lettuce and various root crops grew in the shade of every tree. Her back porch was covered with pots of vegetables and herbs. Her small front yard, however, was a riot of color: roses, shrimp plants, lillies, irises, gardenias, cannas, camellias, azaleas. A banana tree stood on one corner, a Japanese plum tree at the opposite end. There was no grass, just flowers, flowers everywhere.

Eugenia Robichaux and Leola Broussard had been sharing the same part-time gardener, Mr. Moses Washington, for thirty-five years. Mr. Moses was now seventy-five years old and lived with his son and daughter-in-law, who owned a landscaping business and were encouraging him to retire, but Mr. Moses would hear none of it. He told them he would retire when they picked his dead, stiff body up off the ground and placed it in a mausoleum at St. Louis No. 1.

Mr. Moses also practiced voodoo. The Robichaux and Broussard gardens were peppered with little brightly colored scarecrows stuffed with Spanish moss that bore a remarkable resemblance to voodoo dolls, but they kept the birds away and the gardens flourished, so both ladies ignored the dolls and enjoyed their year-round harvests. In New Orleans, hot summers stretch five or six months, autumn melts into spring, and sometimes there is no winter in between, so the city enjoys a twelve-month growing season.

Eugenia hummed along to a CD of Cajun songs given to her by her daughter, Nadine, who lived across the river with her husband and two children. Eugenia (neé Comeaux) was originally from Breaux Bridge, and even though she had come to New Orleans with her husband Michel forty-five years earlier, she still spoke with a Cajun accent and she still loved everything that grew in the ground. She also loved cats.

Eugenia had seven cats, all fixed, all dearly loved and cared for. Thirty years ago Michel had built a two-story, carpeted cat house next to the water heater on the back screened porch where several generations of cats had since resided, surrounded by potted plants, during the few weeks of winter. Most winter days were tolerably warm, but the nights sometimes got down below freezing and Eugenia fretted about the cats until Michel built them their own house. It was soundly built of cypress, with a real roof, and was still in excellent shape, but the carpet had been replaced several times over the years.

Michel retired last year after forty years with the Post Office. Upon retirement, he took it upon himself to instruct Eugenia on how to more efficiently run her house. After two days of life with "Mr. Clipboard", Eugenia told Michel he could either find something to do and get out of her hair or find another place to live. He now drove a cab part-time, went hunting with his Blue Tick hound Tigger as often as possible, and Eugenia continued to run her house full-time. Everybody was happy, especially Tigger.

It was with Tigger that Eugenia was now having an earnest conversation about food. "Yeah, Tigger, we gonna have good eatin' tonight, boy. We got us some softshell crabs over there, and we got us some fried sweet potatoes — you knows ole Michel, he like those fried sweet potatoes — and we got us some pole beans with some Andouie sausage in there and some smothered pork chops. I put extry Zatarain's in the beans this time, spice it all up. Not like that stuff we was give that time over next door by the Yankee people's house. Hoowee! That there was some sorry stuff, Tigger! Plain rice with no tomato gravy, no beans poured over it, nothin'! Just a little butter in there. Tasted like library paste to this ole gal. And them pole beans was just like they come outta the can with some black pepper sprinkle on 'em. Them was *bad*. No hot sauce on the table neither, cher. At least with hot sauce I coulda drowned the taste. But I think the worst was that meat. I doan know for sure *what* that stuff was. She call it a roast, but I doan know a roast *what*. Tasted like roast side 'a the barn to me. And them biscuits. Son, Mr. Mickey Mantel wouldda loved them baseballs! I ate enough to feed a baby bird an' tole her I was on a diet. But just when I thought I was gonna get outta that place with my life, here she comes with dessert. Oh, Tigger, you lucky you still got ole Eugenia with you today. That stuff like to done me in. It was some kinda cake on the bottom and s'pose to be butterscotch pudding on the top and some a' that spray cream outta the can. Runny stuff. I didn't think nobody could mess up pudding, but she sure managed to do just that. It tasted *burnt*. And that cake on the bottom. Lord help us, it tasted like furniture polish mixed in with oatmeal. She call it butterscotch rum cake, but it don't taste like no rum cake. Me, I think she reach for the wrong bottle and mix up the Pledge with the rum. You know what,

Tigger? People who cook like that oughtta just order pizza."

Tigger laid on the floor and made no comment.

*****

Marsha Fellows sat in her kitchen and looked at her stove with absolute loathing. At the moment, it was the focal point of her misery. Because after two years of high school home economics, after purchasing forty different cookbooks, and after watching umpteen hours of cooking shows, Marsha still could not boil an egg without burning it. And for the last year she had been living down south in a culture she did not understand, trying to cook food that she couldn't stand to eat.

Soon after their arrival in New Orleans, Marsha and Graham had gone to a crawfish boil, and Marsha had bravely tried to eat one of those little "mudbugs", but when some drunk redneck had shouted at her to "suck da head and pull da tail," she had thrown the little orange creature onto the ground and run off to hide in the car. Graham, on the other hand, had had a wonderful time, cheerfully washing down crawfish with enormous go-cups of beer and eating boiled vegetables so soaked in hot spice that she'd burnt the roof of her mouth on one of those fiery artichoke hearts.

After the crawfish disaster, Marsha had tried to cook native dishes, she really had, but since she'd never even eaten any of this stuff before, she had no idea how it was supposed to taste, much less any idea how it should be cooked. She now sat and looked at the loathsome stove, sniffling and feeling sorry for herself, and cursing Graham for dragging her down here to the end of the earth where people actually *ate alligator*.

Part of Marsha's culinary problem was that not only did she have little imagination, she also never really followed a recipe. She believed that pork was bad for you, so she always omitted it, and in a city where pork is used to flavor absolutely everything from red beans to turnip greens, if you're going to leave out the pork, you should just give up and eat frozen dinners. Marsha also didn't really believe what she read. If a recipe for red beans and rice called for cooking the beans five hours, she thought it must be a typo and proceeded to cook her beans for fifty minutes. Without pork. Consequently, her beans tasted like boiled beebees. When a recipe called for frying green tomatoes in a cornmeal batter, she decided that nobody *really* ate green tomatoes, and she wasn't fond of cornbread, so she lightly dusted some red tomato slices with flour and threw them into a pan sprayed with PAM. The result looked like something from "Night of the Living Dead". Marsha ate a lot of carryout. Graham was rarely home, so his wife really had no idea what he ate. They ate at home together once or twice a week at best, often separate carryout meals, never ate out together and certainly never had company, since Marsha hated absolutely every living, breathing organism in the State of Louisiana. Except for the night they'd had the neighbors from next door over for dinner. The meal was, predictably, a disaster, and as soon as Mr. and Mrs. Robicheaux had made their escape, Graham had stomped out the house after pitching the entire (mostly uneaten) dinner into the trash, plates and all, declaring it hazardous waste. He then drop-kicked the trashcan out the kitchen door into the side alley. As Marsha listened to his car roar off down the street, she cursed him and fervently hoped he would not return. She got her wish, at least for a few days. Graham finally showed up late Tuesday evening, slightly inebriated, carrying a box of Popeye's chicken.

In her defense, Marsha was not completely at fault for her lack of culinary expertise or her attitude about southern Louisiana, which she considered a foreign country. Marsha was simply the product of her environment.

Marsha had been raised in upstate New York in a household where boiled potatoes, boiled cabbage and baked codfish were considered fit for human consumption; in Marsha's mother's kitchen, salt and black pepper were considered spices and paprika was looked upon as exotic. And in Marsha's family, "travel" was a car trip to Niagra Falls or Lake Placid. These were not adventurous people.

Before her husband had been offered a job at Tulane University, Marsha had never been further south than Washington, D.C. She had gone to college at Penn State, where she had met and married Graham, who soon accepted an assistant-professor position at Dartmouth College in Hanover, New Hampshire, where he later achieved tenure as a professor of economics.

Most of their married life was spent in Hanover, and although Graham traveled extensively, and often, Marsha rarely strayed far from home. She was not an adventurous soul. She and Graham had taken a cruise to Bermuda once long ago, and she had accompanied her husband to conferences in New York City and Boston in the early years of their marriage, but Marsha did not like to fly, nor did she like to travel more than a day's drive from her house. She had once asked Graham to take a car trip with her up to Maine, but he had replied that (a) he did not drive to anyplace he could fly to, (b) there was nothing in Maine that could not be found in New Hampshire, and (c) he would not be living in New England at all if he did not have a wonderful job that allowed him time for extensive travel far, far from Hanover. He then threw her the car keys and told her to drive up to Maine herself, which of course she didn't because she did not like to travel alone. Graham, however, traveled alone a couple of times a month, visiting exotic locales like Miami, San Francisco, Los Angeles, Phoenix, Las Vegas and New Orleans. In twenty years of marriage, Marsha and Graham had taken exactly five trips together.

An insular life in a small New England college town, with little travel to more colorful locations, had ill prepared Marsha for New Orleans, Louisiana. Before moving south, Marsha had imagined New Orleans to be a small, genteel city full of white people where everybody spoke with a southern accent, much like films she had seen set in Charleston, South Carolina and Savannah, Georgia. She also mistakenly thought everybody in New Orleans spoke French. What she found instead was a big, noisy city full of black people she could not understand and white people who all sounded like they were from New York City. The only people she encountered who spoke French were completely unintelligible in either French *or* English, like the people next door. She never understood much of what they were saying, but because she didn't want to look stupid and ask them to repeat themselves, she acted like she understood them and tried to make conversation as best she could. Consequently, she came off as a bit retarded.

Marsha was also completely unprepared for a culture that was definitely not North American. She didn't know what it was, though; she knew of nothing to compare it with. If Marsha had been a bit more worldly, she would have discovered that even though New Orleans is a little like New York and San Francisco, it is more Latin American or Caribbean; however, it is so thoroughly unique that it cannot really be compared to anywhere else in the world.

Marsha's first Mardi Gras was a revelation, to say the least. She had never seen such insanity in all her life. Graham had grudgingly made the mistake of taking her to the French Quarter for some of the festivities, not a good place for someone like Marsha to spend her first Mardi Gras. She saw drag queens fornicating in the streets, bare breasted girls hanging over balconies, X-rated costumes and behavior everywhere. She discovered there were no open container laws in the city, so everyone carried drinks in plastic cups all over town. She was one of the few people who wasn't drunk, and she was one of the few people who wasn't happy. Never having been much of a party person anyway, Marsha emerged on Ash Wednesday dazed and shell-shocked, suffering from something like post-traumatic stress syndrome. Graham emerged with a hangover and a pair of red sequined crotchless panties, which he hung on his car mirror.

Just when Marsha thought all the revelry was over and things would get back to some semblance of normal, St. Patrick's Day arrived and the insanity began all over again, at least for one weekend. At the Irish Channel parade she decided, as cabbages and potatoes whizzed past her head, that she would never understand people who threw vegetables from floats. She also decided that New Orleans would never be what she called normal — to her it was one big lunatic asylum. Look at her neighbors.

*****

Graham Fellows sat at the corner, drumming his fingers on the steering wheel of his red classic 1956 Ford Thunderbird, staring down the street at his wife's white two-door Saturn. The woman had no imagination whatsoever, even in her choice of cars. Graham put his head down on the steering wheel and decided that he simply could not bear the thought of having dinner with her tonight. Not that Graham spent much time at the house he ostensibly "shared" with Marsha, but he just couldn't face even one more night of listening to Mozart or Bach while they ate take-out Chinese food. Not one more night of listening to Marsha whine about how she hated everything about New Orleans, how weird the neighbors were, and she just wanted to go back to New England. He decided to pack her scrawny, whiny little white ass off to her parents in Albany, New York as soon as possible. Bringing her down here had definitely been a mistake.

Graham made two calls from his cell phone, the first to Marsha to tell her he had two meetings to attend and he wouldn't be home until late, and the second to his girlfriend in the Quarter to tell her to get ready, he was taking her to dinner at Sbisa's. Then he rounded the corner, got back out on St. Charles Avenue and headed straight to the Quarter, straight to Isabella.

Graham had been sharing a condo in the French Quarter with Isabella Fairchild for the past sixteen years. They had met in a bar in the Quarter eighteen years earlier, when Graham was in New Orleans for a convention. Isabella was not only a statuesque blonde beauty, she was also funny and feisty, and she loved wild, kinky sex. Isabella did things in bed that Marsha had never even *heard* of (Marsha's idea of getting wild in bed was to get on top).

When Graham first met her, Isabella was the young widow of a very wealthy New Yorker who had been fifty-two years older than her. She had proven to him that he could still get it up, and he had gratefully married her then left her all his money when he died six years later. She had moved back home to New Orleans and had been gleefully spending her late husband's money ever since.

Two years after meeting Isabella in hotels in five different countries, Graham's grandfather died and left him a not-so-small fortune. Graham neglected to inform Marsha of his windfall, put the money in an offshore account, and bought a beautiful condo in the Quarter with Isabella. They had been sharing a life there ever since.

A year after they bought the condo, Isabella introduced Graham to Vicky, a cute little redhead whose affections they shared for the next nine months. Since that time, Isabella had introduced Graham to Maria, Nancy, Lizette, Teresa, Francine and a few girls whose names he couldn't remember. Graham knew there were several girlfriends Isabella had *not* shared with him, but he never pressed her about her life without him; he was just grateful for the time they had together. Now that he was living in New Orleans full-time, he and Isabella were seriously discussing a more permanent arrangement. Graham desperately wanted to divorce Marsha, had wanted to divorce her since their second week of marriage, when he realized he'd made the biggest mistake of his life.

Graham had married Marsha because she told him she was pregnant. Like a fool, he never insisted on evidence; once they were married, she said she'd made a mistake, she wasn't pregnant after all. When he threatened to leave her, get an annulment, she tried to kill herself by drinking Windex, so he put off leaving her until she could stabilize. She never did stabilize, staged a few more suicide attempts, and here he was, twenty years later, sharing a condo mostly full-time with his mistress and trying to figure out how to divorce his wife. Isabella's solution was probably the best: send her skinny New England butt back to Albany, move his things out of their uptown house, serve Marsha with papers in New York, and then the hell with it. If she staged another suicide attempt, tough shit. At this point he would not even feel remorse if Marsha died, just relief. Isabella was right — Marsha was a spoiled, selfish brat who did whatever it took to get what she wanted.

As Graham was parking his car, he looked down the street at two men in identical white suits and pink shirts walking toward him, and suddenly he knew exactly how was going to get *Marsha* to leave *him*.

*****

Miss Libby Leboeuf turned off her living room light and peeked out her front window from a slit in the curtains. Not late enough yet, too many people still coming and going. She would wait another two or three hours before she went out. It had been two weeks since she'd cut anything down, and she was itching to do some yard work. Charley Byrd's yard was going to hell in a handbasket — it looked like an absolute jungle over there — but she didn't dare touch it. The last time she'd cut down his weeds, he'd gone crazy and dumped eight cans of trash all over her yard. It had taken her all morning to pick up all that garbage. In retaliation, she'd spray painted his truck a nauseating bright pink, which only served to further enrage Mr. Charley. The next morning she'd found her doors caulked shut. Since all her windows had bars, she had to call 911 and get the fire department to come over and get her out of her house. She left Mr. Charley alone after that.

Miss Libby went to her back porch to inspect her weed eater. She put in fresh string and topped off the gas tank, then tested it on her back yard. Miss Libby's grass was always trimmed down almost to the dirt. There were bald patches here and there where she'd gotten a little overly enthusiastic with the weed eater.

Even though Miss Libby had been sued in Small Claims Court five times in the last six years, and even though the police had come to her house three times since Valentine's Day, Miss Libby had barely slowed down her nocturnal pruning. Lately she'd started taking her weed eater to other neighborhoods, but she'd discovered that she couldn't hide from her reputation. The police had found her one morning after she'd styled a few bushes two streets over.

Miss Libby was actually thinking of finding another hobby, though, especially after the last incident two weeks ago, when she left the little willow tree a couple of doors down the street absolutely stripped of foliage, and the Yankee lady had made such a scene that Miss Libby's daughter Julia had threatened to put her away someplace where she would never be able to touch another weed eater as long as she lived. Julia told her it was no way for a seventy-three-year-old woman to act and besides, she was tired of paying her court costs. After that Julia had insisted on taking her to Our Lady of Sorrows Senior Center, where she was learning to knit and crochet. Julia hoped it would take her mother's mind off weed whacking.

The night after the willow tree incident, Miss Libby had asked Carlos Espinoza, who lived behind her, if she could buy one of his chickens, preferably deceased but intact. When she explained why she wanted the chicken, he handed over a big black and orange bird with a grin and said "no charge." Carlos had been at odds with that ugly Yankee lady ever since she'd called the police during one of his ceremonies in his back yard. She told the cops that he was torturing animals and howling. Luckily, Carlos' cousin Danny Santos was the officer sent out to investigate. Danny told Mrs. Fellows that there was no law against draining the blood out of a *dead* chicken and that Carlos had been singing not howling, and besides, there was no known law against either singing or howling in one's own back yard before ten o'clock at night. So when a recently-expired chicken was discovered affixed to the door knocker of the Yankee people's house the morning after the willow tree incident, the police told Mrs. Fellows that there was also no law against leaving a dead chicken hanging from a door knocker. When Mrs. Fellows started screaming and threw the chicken into the front yard, the policeman advised her to try to get along with her neighbors and by the way, if she didn't want that chicken, he'd like to take it home with him, he was going alligator hunting the next day. She told him to stick the chicken up his ass and slammed the door in his face.

Miss Libby decided tonight she'd better go further down the street with her weed eater, just to keep peace on the block. She'd noticed an Oleander hedge three blocks away that could use some trimming. She put her weed eater on the back porch and went inside to pass the time by watching the Home and Garden channel. She didn't want to miss the garden design show — tonight they were demonstrating the fine art of clipping hedges into animal shapes.

*****

Donnie Lee Bergeron was dancing around his bedroom to a Gloria Estefan CD, busily turning himself into Donna Damone. He was in an absolute tizzy over what to wear to the annual Delta Queens Masquerade Ball. It was *tonight*, for heaven's sake! (Donnie Lee was the king — or queen — of procrastinators.) Two years ago he went as a bride, when he was still with that rat fink Reggie, who later ran off to Miami with a little Brad Pitt look-alike. Absolute trash, both of them. Last year he and Gerald went as Scarlet and Rhett, but this year Gerald was going as Fred Astaire, so Donnie Lee really had no choice but to go as a movie star. He made a very credible Marilyn Monroe, but he was tired of being Marilyn. After agonizing for another twenty minutes, he finally decided on his flaming red wig and gold sequined dress. He was going for a Rita Hayworth look, but in truth he looked more like Lucille Ball.

Donnie Lee had lived with his mother, Cordelia, all his thirty-nine years until her tragic death two years ago. He had been devoted to her, had taken care of her ever since she had slipped in a puddle of beer at the bingo parlor and hit her head (she'd never been the same afterward and kept calling him Arnie, which was the name of a Pekinese they'd had years earlier). But then a freak accident had taken her away. Donnie Lee never really understood how his pet gerbil, Tillie, got out of her cage and down his mother's throat and choked her, but the coroner surmised it must have happened while Cordelia was snoring. For a long time Donnie Lee blamed himself for her death — maybe if he had been home instead of partying with the boys at Cowpokes he could have saved her. But alas, he had been out dancing in his hot pink satin boxer shorts and purple cowboy boots while his dearly beloved mother was breathing her last. He would never really forgive himself.

Donnie Lee pulled the gold dress over pantyhose and falsies, then straightened the wig on his small, angular head. He carefully applied a heavy layer of makeup, false eyelashes and fire engine red fake nails, then stepped into three-inch gold highheels. He was reaching for his gold and white feather boa when Gerald rang the doorbell with his silver-tipped cane.

Gerald was a perfect date. He presented Donnie/Donna with a box of Godiva chocolates and a sheaf of long-stemmed red roses, fastened a diamond tennis bracelet around his/her dainty wrist (Donnie Lee was a short man with small bones), then led his powdered and perfumed date to his rented stretch limousine. They sat in the back seat and sipped champagne all the way to the ball, where they arrived in splendor and slightly intoxicated. Grover, the black two-hundred-fifty-pound former heavy-weight boxer in the driver's seat, promised to retrieve them at three a.m., then climbed back into the front seat and headed across town to spend some quality time with Juanita. "You the real thang, baby," he muttered to himself. "No false boobiess, no fake eyelashes, and no dingaling between yo' legs."

*****

Jimmy Jackson pulled up in front of his grandmother's house and immediately killed the engine, then removed *Big Willy* from the tape deck and stuck it under the seat. On second thought, he also stashed his magazine under the seat, the one with the picture of Louis Ferrakhan on the cover. He didn't want to go through another exorcism. The last time his grandmother, Miss Minnie Jackson, saw him reading an article about Louis Ferrakhan, she thought he was getting ready to join the Black Muslims and had the priest come over to pray the devils out of him. When he bought incense from the Purple People on Canal Street, Miss Minnie threw it on the ground and screeched like a barn owl and told them they were all possessed by the demons of hell. She was so upset her wig was quivering. She took a swipe at one of the Purple Girls with her big old purse, but luckily she missed. When the girl told her she'd pray for her, his grandmother hollered, "Don't you pray for me, you little purple hussy!" Then she carried on all the way down Canal Street, fussing about the Purple People making bombs over on Magazine Street. According to Miss Minnie, they were all a bunch of Ethiopian terrorists trying to take over the Irish Channel by way of the Jackson Avenue ferry. While Jimmy was mentally trying to work that one out, his grandmother did a one-eighty and started in on the music industry, declaring rap and hip-hop to be the work of Satan. She ranted on about Master P until Jimmy reminded her that she'd known him since he was six — she went to church with his grandmother. She stopped and smiled and said oh yes, Percy was a good boy, but look at what happened to his brothers, they were a tragedy, and Jimmy could not disagree. By the time he dropped her off at her house, Jimmy desperately needed a drink. Any outing with Grandmamma was exhausting.

Jimmy sighed and steeled himself for the next couple of hours. On Wednesday and Saturday nights he took Grandmamma to mass, and every time Jimmy appeared at the door, Grandmamma asked where Alice was. Jimmy always patiently explained that Alice preferred to go to mass alone, but the truth was that his fiancé absolutely refused to go to mass with Miss Minnie — or just about anywhere else, for that matter.

Alice said an evening with Jimmy's grandma was a three-Valium event. She was right, of course. Jimmy knew his grandmother was nuts, but she had raised him, been there for him when nobody else wanted him, had put him through Xavier Prep and Dillard. She even helped him find his first job with the City. Everything he had he owed to that nutty little eight-six-year-old woman with the bad wig. So if she wanted him to take her to mass twice a week, then he took her to mass twice a week. He also bought her groceries on Saturday afternoons, cooked her dinner on Sundays, and took her to her regular Tuesday morning doctor appointments. He paid for her live-in companion, Dorothea, who was good to her and (blissfully) half deaf. He also paid all of his grandmother's bills, everything from utilities to taxes, which wasn't a great deal, since her house was long since paid for and Medicaire picked up her medical bills. He insisted that she use her Social Security and her pension money for herself. Grandmamma called Jimmy her "angel", and he was.

Jimmy and Alice were getting married next month and were in the process of furnishing the house they had bought on Chestnut Street. They did not currently live together because his grandmother and her father would have had simultaneous heart attacks at the mere suggestion of such a thing. So they were getting married and going to Aruba for their honeymoon and *then* moving into their beautiful eighty-year-old home, which they hoped to fill with beautiful children. For now they had his Afghan, Max, and her Greyhound, Oprah.

Jimmy had met Alice at Charity Hospital, where he was being treated for wounds he received in Audubon Park. He'd been jogging early one Saturday morning when he was attacked, for some bizarre reason, by a goose that ran squawking at him from out of the bushes along the lagoon. In the process of trying to defend himself (by trying to throttle the goose), he'd tripped over an oak tree root and knocked himself out. He came to in the Charity Emergency Room, where Alice was treating him for a mild concussion and peck marks on his butt. When he seemed alarmed about the peck marks, she said not to worry, the goose hadn't pecked anything important and she was sure he could still have children. He asked her if she would do him the honor of bearing *his* children. She said sure, so long as you can prove you aren't a lawyer. He said he was an accountant, but she wouldn't go out with him until he had produced a business card, his driver's license and a picture of his grandmother. Alice told him any man who carried a picture of his grandmother in his wallet was either Mr. Wonderful or deeply disturbed. He said why don't you come to dinner with me and find out which category I fit into, so she went to dinner with him on Tuesday night and discovered that, like most people, he was somewhere in between wonderful and disturbed.

Jimmy sighed again, checked his car to make sure there was nothing visible that would offend his grandmother, then went to the door to collect her. After mass he would pick up Alice for a late dinner at the Praline Connection. Early in their courtship, Alice had once suggested that she meet Jimmy somewhere after mass instead of him having to pick her up. He'd been genuinely appalled and told her that a gentleman always picks up a lady at her door. That was when she decided to marry him.

*****

Avery Billiot sat among the pink plastic flamingoes and other assorted faux wildlife in his mother's backyard, offering tobacco to the four directions and saying his evening prayers, when he heard shuffling on the sidewalk next to the yard. He peeked through the bamboo and saw Miss Libby rounding the corner. She was armed.

Avery quickly let himself out the side gate and hurried to the front of the house. Just last month Miss Libby had leveled one of his mother's gardenia bushes, and he wasn't going to let her get a second chance at the rest of the yard. By the time he turned the corner, Miss Libby had revved up the weed eater and was attacking Larry Hebert's asperdistras, which had hitherto lain peacefully under his oak tree next door to the Billiot house. Larry came flying out of his house in his undershorts and a Saints tee-shirt, armed with a broom, and proceeded to whack Miss Libby on the head. She was attempting to give Larry a new haircut with her trusty weed eater while he staved her off with the broom, when Avery grabbed her from behind and wrenched the weed eater away from her. She spit, scratched, kicked and cursed at both of them. Avery yanked the weed eater out of her grasp and banged it against the side of Larry's house until it looked like it had been munched by Godzilla. Miss Libby tried in vain to stop him, but not only was Avery two hundred and ten pounds of solid muscle, he was one pissed off Indian on a mission from God. When Miss Libby saw the remains of her beloved weed eater, she sat on the ground and alternately howled and cried, wringing her hands and pulling her hair. Avery told Larry to watch her while he went inside to call Miss Libby's daughter.

Just as Avery opened the front door, Livonia Billiot came out of her bedroom in her orange mumu and braids and wanted to know what the devil was going on.

"Miss Libby is mourning the death of her weed whacker. I killed it." While Avery went to the kitchen to phone Julia, Livonia went outside to try to keep peace.

When Avery got Julia out of bed to hear, once again, that Miss Libby was on the rampage, Julia muttered "fuck" a few times, then agreed to come see about her mother. After Avery told her the story of the weed eater's demise, and Miss Libby's reaction, Julia decided to bring her brother Francis, an ex-wrestler turned hairdresser.

Avery hung up the phone and went back outside, where his mother was sitting next to Miss Libby on the ground, talking in her soft, sing-song voice. "Libby, you got to cut this out. They gonna put you away, you not careful. You're too old for this shit. Being crazy is a luxury none of us can afford. You obsessed. The witches done got to you."

Miss Libby looked at Livonia and asked, rather pitifully, "Do you think I'm crazy?"

"I don't think you really crazy, Libby, I just think you got nothing else to do. When Jeremy died, you sat around and cried for six months, then you took up with this here weed whacker. You feel like nobody loves you, so you gonna cut down everything that's beautiful, everything that's alive. That's what I think."

Miss Libby blinked up at Larry. "I'm sorry I attacked you. You scared me."

Larry nodded. "It's okay. I'm sorry I hit you with the broom."

Livonia told Miss Libby they would walk her home, so they all trooped down the street. Livonia said she would wait in the front parlor with Miss Libby until Julia and Francis arrived. Avery couldn't leave his mother there to walk home alone — it was one-thirty in the morning — so he sat down in a big wing chair and immediately started snoring. Larry went home and crawled into bed, where he'd been when all the commotion started.

*****

Lucille Fontenot finished *The Muff Murders* and went to the kitchen to get another Barq's rootbeer. She still wasn't sleepy, so she turned on the TV in the second parlor; there was always something on cable. Somebody on HBO was being devoured by giant worms, there were naked people in a taxi on Showtime, and Cinemax was having a Godzilla marathon. She switched to the Food Network, where a young oriental man was frying eels in peanut oil. She sighed and turned off the TV. Ninety-eight channels and nothing on but trash.

Lucille turned out her lights and peeked out the front door curtain. She saw Livonia, Avery, Larry (in his undershorts) and Miss Libby headed down the street. She wondered what they were doing out at that hour but she didn't want to go out on the porch in her nightgown to find out. She knew Mr. Charley wouldn't be trash diving tonight because tomorrow wasn't a trash day, but even on his off nights he sneaked around the neighborhood in a camouflage hunting jacket, doing what he called "reconnaissance". She didn't think he peeked in anybody's windows — he wasn't perverted, just crazy. He sneaked through his neighbors' back yards, though, which occasionally got him in trouble.

Lucille would never forget the night Mr. Charley got hung up in Eugenia's merliton vines. He'd been sneaking through the Robichaux back yard with his flare gun when he stepped on Tigger, who'd been peacefully sleeping in the watermelon patch off the back porch. Tigger jumped up and howled, throwing Mr. Charley to the ground. Mr. Charley dropped the flare gun, which went off and sent up a flare over the Yankee people's house, waking up the Yankee lady, who thought the neighborhood was under attack and ran out of her house in her little blue nightie, screaming that the Cubans had bombed her house. (Graham was, at that moment, sharing a pitcher of margaritas with Isabella on a beach in the Yucatan and missed all the excitement.)

Marsha's screams brought Carlos Espinoza running from his house with his shotgun, which only served to confirm Marsha's conviction that Cubans *were* attacking New Orleans. It didn't help that Carlos' t-shirt was speckled with chicken blood from the latest sacrifice. By the time Carlos shouted, "Shut the fuck up, lady," Marsha was babbling incoherently and curled into the fetal position under her banana tree.

In the meantime, Mr. Charley had tried to run through the Robichaux back yard and had become hopelessly entangled in Eugenia's merlitons, which covered the clothesline that crisscrossed one side of the yard. Tigger, the sweetest of all God's creatures, ran over to try to help Mr. Charley and somehow managed to get his paw stuck in the flare gun, sending off another flare, this time over Miss Libby's house (she wasn't home, having sojourned a few blocks away to style a Japanese yew tree). Poor Tigger limped around in circles and bayed mournfully. Eugenia ran out back and removed the flare gun from Tigger's paw, then she disentangled Mr. Charley, fussed at him and told him to quit sneaking around like a weasel, look at all the trouble he'd caused — that Yankee lady would probably have to go off to DePaul's — then took him inside and gave him some gumbo and a cup of coffee. By that time Lucille and Leola were also standing around in Eugenia's back yard, having heard the commotion, so they all sat down in Eugenia's kitchen and ate gumbo.

Eugenia told Mr. Charley if he'd get married again and eat right, maybe get him a dog and go fishing, he wouldn't be sneaking around the neighborhood like that damn Rambo in the movies; he needed to grow up and act his age. "You ain't no secret agent," she scolded. Mr. Charley ate his gumbo and grumbled about how things had changed too much the last twenty years, and now there was so much crime that *somebody* had to make things safe for the neighborhood. Eugenia told him it was too much for one old man — go home and go to sleep like a normal person. They all got home about two-thirty.

Lucille turned out the light and peeked out the side window just in time to see Michael Flaherty tiptoeing down the back steps of the house next door. "Well you little stinker," she muttered. So he was fooling around with that little hussy Jackie Cheramie. And him married to that sweet little Melanie, too. Not that she could really blame Jackie for having no morals — look at her mother — but Michael knew better. Lucille had taught Michael high school history at St. Anthony's, and she knew his parents were fine people with strong values. Well, it just goes to show you, even good people produce offspring who can't keep their underwear on.

Just Off the Streetcar Line

Lucille opened up her Barq's and went in the bedroom to find another book. She sorted through a pile of new mystery novels on the desk and settled into bed with *The Nun Sucker*, a story about a modern-day vampire who had a penchant for nun necks.

*****

Leola Broussard sat stitching a quilt. Leola also suffered from insomnia and usually downed a shot of Johnny Walker Red every night around midnight, which generally did the trick by twelve-thirty, but tonight Johnny Walker had fallen down on the job and Leola was still awake at two-thirty in the morning, making a quilt for her daughter Marjory. Leola had taught home economics at St. Dominic's and could make anything with her hands, but Marjory was an attorney in Atlanta who couldn't make a birdhouse with popsicle sticks when she was in Girl Scouts, and she hadn't changed much since then. Marjory also hadn't developed an interest in marriage, and since she was now thirty-six years old, Leola had long suspected that her only daughter was either gay or having an affair with a married man. She really preferred the former to the latter; being gay was tough, but married men were nothing but trouble. But since Marjory rarely shared her personal life with her mother, Leola was left to speculate.

Leola removed her reading glasses, rubbed her eyes and sighed. At least Marjory was relatively normal. Troy was another story.

Troy Broussard was Leola's thirty-year-old son. She'd had him a little late in life and had lavished him with attention. He was a beautiful child and an excellent student, had never given her any trouble in his teenage years. Went off to LSU and got a degree in forestry, got a good job with Wildlife and Fisheries. Then he'd met the bug lady and joined that nudist colony across the lake. Up to that point, Leola had never imagined there might be a bunch of weirdoes running around naked in the woods of St. Tammany Parish. Now her baby boy was one of the weirdoes and she just couldn't understand where she'd gone wrong. Troy had gone to mass faithfully every Saturday night, had always eaten his vegetables, never drank or smoked or took drugs. But now he was running around with no drawers on in front of God and everybody on the North Shore. Well, not everybody — he still had to keep his pants on to keep his job. But ever since he met that wild girl, that Valerie, he'd been waving his privates in the breeze to all and sundry.

Valerie Vanderhagen was a beautiful blonde entomologist from San Diego, California, which explained absolutely everything to Leola. People from California were strange creatures with no upbringing. Troy had met Valerie two years ago when she moved to Louisiana and took a job with Wildlife and Fisheries. (She said Louisiana had the most fascinating bugs in the United States.) Two months later, she and Troy had shed their clothes and most of their brains and were living in unwedded (and naked) bliss at Sunny Acres. So far Troy had already suffered from sunburn, excessive mosquito bites and damn near frostbite on his previously unexposed body parts. Leola had hoped that all this physical discomfort would bring Troy to his senses and he would put his clothes back on, but so far he was still living in sin out in the woods. Leola sighed and silently blamed her son's shortcomings on Vinnie.

Vinnie Broussard was Leola's long departed first husband who had unexpectedly dropped dead of a freak accident when Troy was four years old. Vinnie was a tugboat captain until that fateful night when he was pushing a load of barges up to St. Louis and had tied up in Memphis for two days. He and his friend Bernard had gone out and gotten drunk and brought a prostitute back to the boat. In his scramble to get laid, Vinnie had somehow managed to get tangled up in the hooker's enormous brassiere and in his haste to free his head had actually hung himself off the side of the boat. When Bernard tried to free his friend from the brassiere's lacey grasp, Vinnie fell into the Mississippi and drowned.

After Vinnie's demise, Leola waited a suitable period of time, then married Vinnie's brother Alfonse, whose wife Della had run off with an encyclopedia salesman from Nashville. Della later ran off with a country singer who subsequently got rich and departed for Caracas with his Venezuelan masseuse. Not to be outdone, Della rallied, got a boob job and a facelift, and moved to Acapulco, where she married a retired matador turned restauranteur.

Alfonse turned out to be boring but faithful, a good provider and a wonderful father figure to his niece and nephew. Three years ago he had retired from Avondale Shipyard; one month later he had a massive heart attack while eating a burger and fries under the golden arches at Tulane and Broad. The franchise had given Leola a certificate that entitled her to free fast food for life, but in the three years since Alphonse's passing, Leola had not been able to bring herself to enter the establishment where her late husband had eaten his last meal.

Leola put away her sewing for the night. Still not sleepy, she wandered into the kitchen, looking for something interesting to eat, but she'd already eaten everything interesting and closed the refrigerator door in disgust. She was searching through the pantry when she heard scratching and mewing on the back porch. She unlocked the back door and held it open for Jezabelle, her neighbor Demetrius' six-year-old gray Persian (Jezabelle mooched from every house in the neighborhood), just in time to see Michael Flaherty sneaking out Jackie Cheramie's back door. "Well you little snake," she muttered. Jezabelle mewed and twitched her tail. "No, not you, Jezzie. You couldn't do anything if you wanted to — your pieces and parts are long gone." She locked the back door and gave Jezabelle a dish of milk, then divided a plate of cold chicken livers for the two of them. Jezzie curled up on a padded kitchen chair, obviously planning to spend the night.

Leola turned out the light and went back to the bedroom and listened to a talk radio host interviewing a man who insisted that he had been captured by aliens and taken to their secret laboratory at the bottom of Lake Pontchartrain, which Leola knew couldn't be true because the lake was too shallow to hide a dump trunk much less an alien laboratory. Leola finally fell asleep while the guy was describing the head alien, who resembled a green neon praying mantis with wings.

*****

Dave Richard sat in his pajamas at his eighteenth century writing table in the little study off his bedroom, flipping through photographs of Boxcar Johnson's house, trying to pick out the ones that were least offensive to a prospective buyer. The outside shots were easy — late nineteenth century home, painted pale lilac with plum trim, deep front porch, nice gingerbread touches, a little under two thousand square feet of living space. He looked at a nice shot of the bright red front door. It gave no clue as to what was waiting past the threshold.

The interior of Boxcar's house could only be described as Nouveau Voodoo African Mexican Bordello. Dave had never seen anything like it, and he had seen plenty of decorating disasters in his professional lifetime. Boxcar's house was in a class by itself. Every room was a different color, and the colors ran toward the bright and fruity: blueberry, raspberry, cherry, banana, tangerine, plum. But that was just paint

— walls could be repainted (although the interior of Boxcar's house would require at least three coats of paint). The real problem would be showing the house while Boxcar's décor was still on display.

Dave had no idea where his client had purchased his indescribable furniture, rugs, curtains, glassware, paintings, sculpture, lamps, knick-knacks, etc., but he suspected Boxcar had scoured every flea market, thrift store and yard sale between Haiti and southeastern Louisiana. The place looked like an international flea market: a gold painted cupid lamp with little dangling prisms stood next to an enormous Mexican silver crucifix hanging beside a moss-stuffed voodoo doll draped in Mardi Gras beads, which looked down upon a statue of an African woman giving birth, which sat on a marble-topped Victorian table with a lyre stand, which stood next to a bright red Judy Jetson-type kidney-shaped velvet sofa sitting on stainless steel tubular legs, which sat on what looked like a real giraffe fur rug. And that was just one section of one room crammed with unique trash—the entire house was similarly gawd-awful. Judging just by the house, Dave assumed that Boxcar grew up in a dumpster behind a Salvation Army Thrift Store that was located next door to a porno movie house. That second floor! Dave closed his eyes and tried to block out the view of Boxcar's second floor, but those were images that would live with him forever.

The second story of Boxcar's camelback, which consisted of two bedrooms and a bath, was one big bordello from hell. The bathroom alone was enough to give anyone permanent diarrhea: neon green walls, bubble-gum pink fixtures, bright red shower curtain adorned with black roses, photos of naked women sitting on the toilet or the bidet, and plastic spiders hanging everywhere—from the ceiling, down the walls, on the doorknob, from the shower curtain rod. The goddamned room was *filled* with spiders of every size and color. There was also a life-sized mannequin in a blonde wig, red scquined tassels and a silver g-string. It was standing next to the toilet that was rigged so that every time you flushed, the mannequin's nipples lit up and she cooed, "Do it again, baby!" The spare bedroom was similarly tacky, with purple walls and green trim, a chandelier made of deer antlers and draped with Mardi Gras beads, bunk beds painted shiny gold and purple, a bar made out of two old Dracula-type coffins, an enormous voodoo doll sitting on a child's plastic rocking horse, and a hat rack festooned with Boxcar's collection of colorful feather boas. On the walls were pictures of Gene Autry, Dr. John as the Night Tripper, Milton Berle in drag, John Wayne, Mae West, Jackie Robinson, Martin Luther King, Jr., and the current mayor of New Orleans. The whole room had sort of a campy wild west-voodoo-Hollywood look to it. Ugly as sin, of course, but like the rest of the house, original Boxcar. And not nearly as revolting as Boxcar's bedroom.

Boxcar's boudoir looked like a porno nightmare: a huge four-poster bed from which dangled enough ladies' undergarments to stock Macy's lingerie section (souvenirs, no doubt); a tall slender pink chest filled with sex toys (not that Dave snooped — each drawer was clearly labeled as to the accoutrements within); an assortment of fur-lined handcuffs piled on one of the nightstands, along with a leather paddle and a roll of electrical tape; pictures of naked women *everywhere*, all shapes, colors and sizes, in a variety of provocative poses; mirror tiles above the bed and an honest-to-God trapeze dangling from the ceiling; a naked blow-up doll was floating in a corner, tethered to a mechanical bull; and the big-screen TV on the wall facing the bed was flanked by floor-to-ceiling shelves filled with enough porno movies to make Larry Flynt jealous. A giant purple plastic penis sat in the middle of the floor. Dave had looked around with his mouth hanging to his knees, muttering "gawd-almighty" over and over; he decided against any attempt to photograph the room in a favorable light. Dave figured he was doing penance for his wild college years and left the house feeling like he needed a shower. He sat in his car and prayed to whatever real estate saints might be listening, because it was going to take a miracle to sell that house!

As he flipped through one hideous photo after another, Dave shook his head in wonder and disgust. He had tried to photograph from the least bilious angles, but it was virtually impossible not to include five or six revolting objects in each photo. Dave thought of airbrushing the photos, but he decided that prospective buyers might as well be forewarned before they visited Boxcar's house. He decided to very carefully screen buyers for this particular house — no yuppies, born-again Christians or old people with heart problems. He was quite certain that whoever finally bought Boxcar's house would perform an exorcism before moving in anyway. Dave just wanted to prevent a lawsuit before Hell House went to act of sale.

*****

Jackie Cheramie kissed Michael goodbye and quietly closed the back door. She glanced at the kitchen clock and decided to ditch school tomorrow. She needed some sleep – Michael had stayed much longer than expected and had been quite athletic. She would write herself an excuse the next day and sign her mother's name; she'd been doing it for years. Nobody cared, anyway; graduation was within winking distance, and Jackie was at the top of her class. She'd have to get caught having sex with a nun *and* a priest on Canal Street to get thrown out of school at this late date. She idly wondered if Lisa would call home during her jaunt to Las Vegas, but she rather doubted she would hear from her mother. It would've been out of character. Lisa did not tend to think past her pretty little nose.

Jackie turned on her computer and checked her bank balances. Over four thousand in checking; better then forty thousand in one savings account, a little over sixty thousand in another; seventy-one thousand in her money market account. She also had two fifty thousand dollar CD's, plus the money her grandmother had left her in trust, which had come to her last November, when she turned eighteen. Jackie had been playing the stock market for the last couple of years, and she had done very well for a teenage girl still in high school. She had a good broker whom she trusted, but she also had good solid ideas about how to invest her money. Lisa had no idea what their financial situation was, and Jackie deliberately kept her in the dark for her own good.

Jackie had been taking care of the family finances since she turned fifteen, when she discovered that her mother simply could not count. She also discovered that her mother could not be trusted with credit cards, rarely remembered to pay bills, and was easy prey for a host of slick, good looking male predators. So at age fifteen Jackie became legally emancipated, took over all their financial affairs, and completely ran the household. First she paid all the bills that had been gathering dust on top of the desk, then she took away all of Lisa's credit cards and put her on an allowance. Lisa was completely incapable of taking care of herself. It was for this reason that Jackie, who could've had her pick of prestigious universities, had decided to stay in New Orleans and attend Tulane, which is also a very good university, "southern ivy league". Jackie was quite certain that she would never use her degree anyway — she intended to keep making a living in the stock market and retire very early in life, she just thought she might enjoy college. And until she could think of something better to do with her time, college would fill up the hours. Besides, it was a good way to meet men.

Jackie Cheramie was so brilliant that she could have gotten an MBA from Princeton or Yale or Harvard, secured an excellent job in the city of her choice, and probably become head of a major company before age forty. But living in a high rise apartment, donning a little gray suit and black heels, and going downtown to race on a treadmill career track every day in some city like Chicago or New York or Boston was not the way Jackie wanted to live her life.

Like most native New Orleanians, Jackie wanted to live in the city of her birth until she drew her last breath. And she had no intention of working very hard, ever. She lived in a nice house in a nice neighborhood where she was comfortable. She had family and friends and a very satisfying life right where she sat. And right where she sat, she was capable of making more money that she would ever make on a career path, living somewhere else.

In spite of her tender years, Jackie knew exactly what she wanted: a happy life. And she had that right now. Her motto was, why fix it if it ain't broke? And of course she could never leave Lisa. Jackie loved her mother, did not consider her a burden and, like the parent of a handicapped child, was resigned to taking care of her for the rest of her life. Jackie figured the furthest she'd ever move was down the street, if that. She assumed that she would someday get married, which did not necessarily mean moving out of her house. After all, she owned the house. Why move just for the sake of moving? And whomever she married would have to accept Lisa as part of the immediate family. Jackie and Lisa were a package deal.

Jackie yawned and stretched. Two-thirty. She wondered how Michael explained these late nights to his wife, then shrugged and turned off the computer. That was his problem. Jackie turned out the light and went to bed.

*****

Charley Byrd was sprawled buck naked in his cracked and duct-taped recliner, feasting on cheese curls, ranch dip and tequila, watching CNN. He occasionally threw a cheese curl at the TV and muttered "lies, all lies." He finally clicked off the power, brushed the orange cheese curl dust from his stomach and tried to rise from the recliner, but his naked butt was stuck to the vinyl. He carefully extricated himself from the grips of the chair, turning over the remains of the tequila onto the truly ugly piece of orange carpet under the TV tray. The spreading tequila stain joined a host of older stains (coke, coffee, chili, beer, cheese dip). Mr. Charley bemoaned the lost quarter cup of tequila but barely noticed the stains as he ambled toward his bedroom to dress himself. He pulled a pair of green work pants and a tan cotton shirt from a jumbled pile of clothing thrown over an aluminum deck chair. He wandered into the kitchen to retrieve his underwear from the oven, where it had been drying for the past thirty minutes. There were only a couple of scorch marks this time (some of Mr. Charley's underwear had actually caught fire once and smoked up the already dingy kitchen). Mr. Charley usually took his laundry to Suds and Buds, a tavern/laundry a few blocks away, but whenever he ran out of underwear, and he was in a hurry, he washed out a few pairs of ancient boxer shorts and dried them in the oven, with mixed results.

Mr. Charley slung his nightly gear around his neck (army-issue field glasses, a flashlight and a canteen filled with Dixie beer), pulled on his battered running shoes, turned out the kitchen light and quietly slipped out the back door. He blew his stealthy exit by tripping over the sack of trash he'd collected the night before and left sitting on the back porch. He tumbled down the three back steps, landing with an "omph" in the weedy back yard. When he tried to get up, he discovered his canteen was entangled in one of the dozen or so fishing rods leaning against the house. The rods fell with a clatter against the metal bass boat laying under the fig tree. In trying to fight the fishing rods, Mr. Charley fell against the shrimp net hanging from the old clothesline posts. He and the fishing rods became hopelessly entangled in the net, making such a ruckus that Gino Delacroix, who lived behind Mr. Charley, came running through the hole in the fence that separated their back yards.

Gino had been squatting down in the middle of his little vegetable garden, peacefully burying money stashed in a molasses bucket and adjusting his alligator skull markers, when he heard the racket and ran into the yard to find Charley Byrd thrashing and cursing under the fig tree. Gino helped disentangle his neighbor from the shrimp net and fishing poles, then sat down on the back steps with him while Mr. Charley drank beer from his canteen to calm his nerves.

"What the hell you doin' now, my frien'? Sneakin' aroun' like James Bond again, huh?"

Mr. Charley grunted and wiped his mouth on this sleeve. "I was just gonna take a walk."

"With them binoc'lars? Whacha gonna look at this time a' night, the moon? You weren't gonna look in no winders, was you?"

Mr. Charley gave Gino a dirty look. "You know I ain't no pervert! I just carry 'em with me in case I need 'em, that's all."

"You know, Charley, one a' these days, somebody gonna think you a prowler and shoot you in the head. You better stop all a' this secret agent bullshit and fin' you somethin' better to do." Gino pulled a partially smoked cigar out of his shirt pocket and relit it meditatively. "When was the last time you was down at the fishin' camp?"

Mr. Charley spat in the weeds. "Aw, I ain't been down to Lake Catherine since last year, when ole Mickey died." Mickey was Mr. Charley's bloodhound, who'd stopped breathing the year before at the age of fourteen. Gino and Charley had buried him under the olive tree at the corner of the yard, where he'd lain every day of his fourteen years.

Gino puffed on his stinky cigar. "So your boat been sittin' here rustin' in the weeds ever since." Mr. Charley nodded, his eyes watering from the cheap cigar fumes. Gino looked at his fluorescent watch. "It's goin' on three o'clock. I'm going frog giggin'. Wanna come?"

Mr. Charley thought a minute, looked at the mess in his back yard, then nodded again. "Okay. But I need more beer." They went inside to retrieve a six-pack and a set of waders, then got in Gino's 1952 Ford pickup truck and headed east.

*****

Louie Bourgeois passed Gino and Charley as they headed down Magazine Street toward the Mississippi River bridge. Louie vaguely wondered what his neighbors were up to that time of morning, but he didn't dwell on it; he was too busy following Harry Frilot's wife, Betty. Harry sold heavy equipment for oil rigs, which required his presence out in the Gulf at least twice a month, and Harry suspected Betty of infidelity while he traveled. He didn't have any proof, just a hunch. Louie took Harry's money without telling him that Betty had paid Louie to follow Harry about six months earlier. In his files, Louie had three-by-five color shots of Harry and an extremely well endowed blonde doing deep knee bends at a motel in Houma. When Louie had presented Betty with the photos, her only words were, "How does she hold up those things without a crane?" Then she paid Louie and left. Louie suspected that Betty was now practicing full blown retaliation.

That evening Louie had followed Betty from her three-bedroom bungalow a few streets away from Louie's own house to a bar in the suburbs called Foreplay. The place was packed and smoky; Louie had no trouble hiding in the crowd while he watched Betty.

Betty Frilot was a good looking fifty-year-old woman with a trim figure and dark auburn hair, but Louie had never thought of her as anything really special. Tonight he changed his mind. Tonight Betty was wearing a platinum blonde wig, a tight red minidress, dangling red earrings and red high-heeled pumps. She was definitely a knockout, and he wasn't the only guy at Foreplay who thought Betty was something special. After several dances with obvious losers, Betty finally found someone she considered worthy of her attention, a tall handsome man about her age. After bumping and grinding their way around the floor for about forty-five minutes they left, with Louie trailing after them. Betty got into her car and followed Mr. Right to an apartment building not far from the nightclub. Louie parked at a convenience store across the street and waited until they'd gone inside the building. When lights came on in the front apartment, he parked his car at a closed dry cleaners next door and walked across the street and listened at what he assumed was a bedroom window. When he heard enough to be certain of what was going on inside, he walked back across the street to his car and waited. About an hour later Betty left loverboy's apartment and drove her car back to uptown New Orleans, with Louie following.

Louie liked Betty and completely understood what she was doing. He did *not* like her husband Harry. He would take his money, but he didn't like him at all. The guy was a sewer rat. So Louie parked his car in front of Betty's house and walked up her driveway. She let out a little squeak when she got out of her car and saw Louie standing at her bumper.

"You scared the shit outta me! What in God's name are you doing here?"

Louie leaned against the blue Taurus and said, "Following you."

Betty's mouth dropped open. "What? Why are you following me?"

Louie signed and pushed his hair back. "Harry paid me to follow you."

Betty narrowed her eyes at him. "Then what the hell are you doing here?"

"I said he paid me to follow you; I didn't say I was going to report anything." Betty just stared at him. "Look, Betty, I'm here because I like you. You're a nice lady and Harry's a bottom feeder."

Betty started to cry. "He has the morals of a warthog in heat." She was frantically searching her purse for a kleenex. Louie handed her his handkerchief. She leaned against the car and continued to cry.

Louie felt helpless. He put his arm around her and steered her to the front porch. "Come on, let's go inside before we attract attention." She got the front door open and he followed her back to the den. He sat down on the green leather couch while Betty stood in the middle of the room and looked miserable. "I feel slimy," she said.

"Go take a shower, you'll feel better." She just stared at him. "Go on, I'll wait." She nodded her head and left the room. Louie got up and poured two brandies at the little bar in the corner, put a Poncho Sanchez CD in the player, and sat down on the couch to wait. About twenty minutes later Betty returned, damp and wigless, wrapped in a deep blue kimono, wearing just a trace of makeup and some kind of perfume that made him horny as hell. She sat down next to him and sipped a little brandy. Louie thought she looked beautiful and tried not to stare at her nipples protruding through the thin silk robe.

They sat in silence for a few minutes, then Betty turned and looked at Louie. "What are you going to tell Harry?"

Louie looked into her beautiful green eyes and said, "Absolutely nothing." Then he kissed her because he just couldn't help himself. She pulled him down on the couch and he forgot all about Harry for a couple of hours.

*****

Graham Fellows leaned against the headboard of the beautiful Louis XV bed he shared with Isabella Fairchild on Ursuline Street, deep in the heart of the French Quarter. He and Isabella were sharing a bottle of Moet and munching on chocolate-dipped strawberries. After having a truly excellent dinner at Sbisa's, they had gone dancing at Cafe Brazil, where Isabella had removed her black bikini panties on the dance floor and stuffed them in Graham's jacket pocket, a clear signal that she was ready to go home. So Graham took her home, deposited her in the huge clawfoot tub and poured chocolate syrup all over her gorgeous, edible body. They were now squeaky clean and discussing Graham's plan.

"What did Victor say?" Isabella asked.

Graham laughed. "His exact words were, 'Oooh, baby, when do we start?'"

Isabella gave a throaty laugh. "He's such a slut. Think it'll work?"

Graham leaned back and lowered a strawberry into his mouth. "Oh, it'll work. If she simply caught me in bed with another woman, she'd just freak out and stage another suicide attempt. This way she'll blow a fuse and actually leave me."

"If you say so."

"I know so. Remember the time I left the pictures of you and me in my coat pocket? Pictures from one of our trips to Paris. Nothing really incriminating. Marsha found them and tried to hang herself, even though I said you were just another professor at the conference."

Isabella sighed and dipped a strawberry. "I remember. She pulled down the chandelier in the den. I didn't think she was that heavy."

"She isn't, it was loose. Unfortunately. Then there was the time she saw a picture of me with that girlfriend of yours, Yvette, about four years ago. We were standing in the doorway of Irene's restaurant; I think Victor took the picture. Anyway, Marsha threatened to throw herself in front of a bus. I didn't bother to explain the photo or try to talk her out of becoming road kill, so she got pissed off and rammed her piece-of-shit car head-on into my Thunderbird! Cost me thirty-four hundred smackers to get it fixed. I told her if she pulled that shit again, I'd run over her myself."

Isabella smiled. "Yvette. She had the prettiest ass. I really miss Yvette; she was wild, an exhibitionist. Liked to do it on the balcony and in front of the open windows We got a few standing ovations from the girls in the condo across the courtyard. She was a little kinky, though – used to beg me to tie her up and paddle her, then spray her down with whipped cream. I made a lot of sundaes with that girl."

"She was the one who liked big, vibrating dildos."

"That was Yvette. Too bad she fell in love on the Internet and ran off to Texas to meet the love of her life. She still e-mails me, says she's happy with Rosalita."

"Who was the girl who liked feet? Was that Bianca?"

Isabella shook her head. "Vicky. She had a thing about painting my toenails, really turned her on. I didn't have to pay for a pedicure for months. Bianca was the brunette who had that midget sidekick, Lester. Remember? She always led him around with a dog leash. He got drunk and fell off the Canal Street ferry and drowned."

"Yeah, I remember now. Poor Lester. I wonder how he got mixed up with Bianca. She was pretty weird."

"*Very* weird. She was into nipple clips and handcuffs and beatings, stuff like that. We couldn't have sex without her throwing me over her knee every fifteen minutes. I mean, I like a good spanking as much as the next naughty girl, but she was way too into pain. My ass was always bruised and my nipples stayed sore all the time. It got old. We didn't last long."

Graham licked chocolate off his fingers. "She was obnoxious. What made you finally ditch her?"

"Well, I didn't ditch her because of the spankings – that was the least of her psychoses. But I abso-bloody-lutely could not deal with the rodents."

"What rodents?"

"Oh, you know, I told you about it. The night she showed up with the gerbils, I told her to stick those little rats up her own butt and hit the road. My fantasies do not include bestiality in any form. I'm not *that* kinky."

"Good riddance," Graham said, swigging from the bottle of champagne.

"Yeah, but she had her attributes."

"Big tits."

"*Huge* tits. Gave good head, too. And she did introduce me to Victor, who is now one of my dearest friends. Which brings us to *your* little drama."

Graham dipped another strawberry in chocolate. "Oh, it'll be more than a little drama, but it should get rid of Marsha once and for all. And it'll be her word against mine that it ever happened, like if it comes up in court or something. I can prove she's crazy if need be. But I think she'll just leave in disgust, with a minimum of agony. Hell, if I do this on Saturday, she should be long gone forty-eight hours from now. You and I can fly to the Dominican Republic; I'll get a divorce, we'll get married. Simple as that."

Isabella laughed and rubbed chocolate on her nipple. "You can finally make an honest woman of me."

Graham grabbed her breast and licked furiously. "God, I hope not. I've had enough of honest women."

Isabella giggled. "Where are we going on our honeymoon, hot stuff?"

Graham looked up at her with chocolately lips. "Hershey, Pennsylvania."

Isabella let out a belly laugh and smeared chocolate on the other nipple. "Lick this, big boy."

As Graham licked chocolate off his lover's luscious body, he knew he would not be going back uptown anytime soon. His first class was not until eleven, and he didn't plan on explaining his whereabouts to Marsha ever again.

*****

When Donnie Lee and Gerald climbed into the limo a little after two, they told Grover to drive around for an hour or so, preferably on the Interstate. Grover, having just bid Juanita a fond adieu, said, "Certainly, sir, uh ma'am. Ya'll!" He slid into the driver's seat and raised the partition, then turned on the radio to a jazz station. He didn't want to know anything about what was happening on the other side of that partition, and he certainly didn't want to hear any of it. He headed north, toward the lake.

On the other side of the opaque glass wall, Donnie Lee and Gerald, already quite intoxicated, sipped champagne, giggled and pawed one another. Donnie Lee's dress was thrown over the champagne bucket and his black silk panties were on Gerald's head. Donnie removed his falsies and put them over Gerald's ears. "You look like Princess Leia," he giggled.

Gerald waggled his champagne flute at Donnie. "No, my *wife* looks like Princess Leia. I look like a tellatubbie."

"There is a strong resemblance." Donnie untied Gerald's bowtie with his red lacquered toes. "Where does she think you are?"

"Performing brain surgery. Removing a wart. I don't really give a shit, neither does she." Gerald was a prominent local surgeon. He and Donnie had met in the Emergency Room one night when Donnie's boyfriend of the moment, Rex, had snorted six lines of cocaine on top of half a bottle of tequila and then had tried to insert the business end of a No. 9 iron into a very vulnerable area of Donnie's anatomy. The ensuing fight had left Donnie with a concussion, along with various bruises and lacerations. Donnie, however, had fought like a tiger, and when the police arrived they found Rex out cold on the living room floor with an empty tequila bottle stuck on the end of his penis and his bloody left nipple pierced with a rhinestone brooch.

Donnie worked on removing Gerald's pants with his toes. He was quite flexible. "Who's she bopping this month?" he asked, referring to Gerald's wife, Rochelle.

"Lennie Lassiter, the guy who did her boobs. I guess she wanted to try them out on a pro."

"What size did she get?"

"Double D's. I think she looks like Dolly Parton on steroids, but she's happy. Next month she's getting a butt lift. The liposuction left her a little saggy in the saddle."

"Why is she rebuilding Atlanta all of a sudden?"

Gerald wiggled out of his black trousers. "Because she's forty-five and bored shitless. She has nothing better to do than spend my money on a new wardrobe, a new car and a new body. Rochelle is the quintessential American female consumer without a budget. On Monday she shops the entire day, breaking only to have lunch and spread malicious gossip with a few select friends. On Tuesday she lays by the pool all day with a pitcher of Bloody Mary's, recovering from Monday. On Wednesday she plays golf. All of Thursday is spent at the Body Boutique, where they do her hair, nails, face, the works. Hell, they probably wax her entire body. Friday she spends at our condo in the Quarter, bopping the flavor of the week. One Saturday a month is spent with our daughter Gillian, shopping and prying into Gillian's life. Other Saturdays are spent with her little wolf pack of friends, doing whatever it is they do – hot air ballooning, gator hunting, dancing naked on Bourbon Street. I have no idea."

Donnie was trying to remove Gerald's jockey shorts with two toes. "Is Gillian still seeing that girl from Covington, the underwear model?"

"Cheryl. Yes, they're still together."

"Does Rochelle know about it yet?"

"Oh heavens no! Rochelle's dyed platinum locks would turn green overnight if she ever found out. She doesn't even know *I'm* gay – she thinks I have a mistress." Donnie giggled and yanked on Gerald's drawers with his toes. "Every time Rochelle presses Gillian about the men in her life, Gillian brings over one of her gay male friends and introduces him as her latest boyfriend. It keeps Rochelle from going into shock." He sighed and removed the panties and falsies from his head. "Thank God I have an honest relationship with my daughter."

Donnie Lee wrapped his legs around Gerald's neck and yanked him to the floor of the limo. "Come down here and have an honest relationship with me, Doctor G."

Just Off the Streetcar Line

They rocked and rolled down I-10 and back again, then instructed Grover to return them to their respective points of origin, which Grover was happy to do. He was even happier with the two hundred dollar tip Gerald bestowed upon him.

*****

Anthony Guidry slipped quietly into the house and tiptoed down the hall to his bedroom. The Guidry house was an old cottage style home, with a hallway running down the middle of the house from the front door to the back. All the rooms opened off the hall. He noticed his sister's bedroom door was closed; she must've stayed overnight. He hoped from the depths of his soul that she had not actually moved back home.

Anthony locked his bedroom door and looked out the window at Jackie Cheramie's house. Rats, he thought, all dark. Sometimes when he came home from the night shift at Sav-a-Center, he caught Jackie still up and prancing around in front of the window in her underwear. He especially liked her purple thong and matching bra. He wondered what it would take to get her into bed. He knew she was promiscuous; he also knew she was having an affair with Michael Flaherty, but that couldn't last forever. Michael was married and he was a weenie.

Anthony sighed and pulled a videotape from under his dresser, turned the volume all the way down on his TV and stuck the tape in the VCR. "Luscious Babes" flashed on the screen, "starring Velvet Dawn,

Kitty Lovely, Dominique Demure and Biff Steel." Anthony watched naked girls with surgically enhanced bodies frolic in a stable, then under a tree and finally in a swimming pool. They were occasionally joined by Biff Steel, who couldn't possibly have a schlong that big, nobody did. Anthony finally turned off the VCR and wandered into his bathroom to take a shower. As he did every night, he measured his pecker, but it was still the same size as it was the night before. Hadn't grown a millimeter. He'd spent $27.95 on a penis enlargement kit, which had involved a little Velcro band, a pump and a suction hose, but it hadn't enlarged anything other than the manufacturer's bank account. He had also tried drinking ginseng tea, which had kept him up all night, and he had ordered various potions found in the back of girlie magazines. He may as well give up and learn to live with the six inches God gave him.

Anthony Guidry was actually a very nice looking young man with an ordinary physique. He was simply under the mistaken impression that girls wanted a man with a donkey schlong. He desperately needed his own apartment and a normal love life. If he didn't get away from his mother soon, he was going to have to throw himself onto the streetcar tracks. He decided to look at the apartment ads in the Sunday paper. All he really needed was one big room.

Anthony walked back into his bedroom and pulled a *Penthouse* from behind his dresser. He looked at pictures of naked women and ads for sex toys until he couldn't keep his eyes open, then fell asleep and dreamed that he was trying to have sex with Kate Winslet on the prow of the Love Boat. Just as things were getting really interesting, he was thrown overboard by Austin Powers, who actually looked a lot like his mother in a bad wig. As he hit the water, he woke up and discovered he'd swept his water glass off the bedside table and dumped it all over himself. He laid a towel on the bed and went back to sleep; this time his dream involved Madonna and pointy pink bras.

*****

Miss Beulah was up at dawn, picking elder flowers for a potion. "Gots to pick 'em right at sunrise, lessen the spell won't work," she muttered to herself, breaking off a stalk just as the sun peeked over the church bell tower down the street. She put the stalk in a gunny sack, then picked as many berries as she could reach and put them in a plastic bucket. Miss Beulah made the best elderberry wine in the parish. She then bent over and picked a dandelion bud just beginning to open and stuck it in the sack with the elder flowers. "Thas right, thas right. Get a dandelion bud at end of night." She hummed softly to herself and hobbled over to the big willow tree in the corner of the back yard. She peeled a little bark from a twig, adding that to her sack as well. She bent over the beans in her little garden and plucked a beetle from a leaf, wrapped a piece of mint around it and crushed it between her thumb and forefinger. "I's sorry about that, Mista Beetle, but I got plans for you." The recently deceased

Mista Beetle and the mint leaf were added to the contents of the sack.

Miss Beulah took her treasures into the kitchen. She dumped the elder berries into a plastic bag and placed them in the freezer next to five other bags of berries. The items in the gunny sack were carefully examined and gently laid in a little cast iron pot sitting on the stove. Miss Beulah then took several glass jars from her pantry. From one she pulled out a dried toad and broke off the end of one of its feet, then put away the rest of the little creature for future use. She then unscrewed the top of a jar labeled "river mud" and measured two teaspoons of the powdery dirt. She removed the cork on the last little bottle and added three drops of patchouli oil. She put the jars back in the pantry, then took a chicken bone wrapped in a tobacco leaf out of the freezer and used the bone to stir the concoction in the pot. She stirred it four times around, clockwise, mumbled some words over it, then threw in the chicken bone and the tobacco leaf.

Miss Beulah took the pot outside and held it up to the fading moon, said a prayer, then dug a hole under the willow tree, poured in the entire contents of the pot, and replaced the dirt. She then took a piece of paper with some numbers written on it and a lighter from her apron pocket. She placed the paper in the pot and set it on fire. When the paper was reduced to ashes, she dumped the ashes on top of the dirt she'd just put in the hole. Then she washed out the pot under the outside spigot and laid it upside down on the back step to dry.

Her ritual finished, Miss Beulah went inside to cook eggs with peppers, apple sausage, cheese grits with crawfish, fried green tomatoes, and buttermilk biscuits. She placed the feast on the dining room table, then added a pot of coffee, a pitcher of milk, a carafe of grape juice, jars of fig preserves and pepper jelly, a pitcher of cane syrup, a bottle of tobasco sauce, and a big jar of pickled watermelon rind and okra. She set the table for five, then went to wake her husband Elijah, her daughter Yolanda, her granddaughter Clarice, and her son Leroy, recently returned to the bosom of his family after paying his debt to society at the parish prison.

*****

Eugenia Robichaux was up at five, picking vegetables and administering to her garden. The cats were up, too, chasing each other around in the dew. Tigger lay under the merlitons, stretching and yawning and scratching himself; he was not normally an early riser.

Eugenia straddled Tigger and picked a small basketful of merlitons. "Got to get me some a' these merlitons, Tigger. Gonna stuff 'em with shrimp for supper." A calico cat mewed at her feet. "I'll give ya'll them shrimp heads, minou. I know my little kitties loves the shrimps." Tigger sneezed several times and the little cat ran for cover. "You got bugs up your nose, ole boy? You done scared Angelica to under the house." Tigger yawned in reply and rolled over on his side.

After Eugenia picked enough pole beans for a pot, a pile of okra, and a half-dozen tomatoes, she leaned over under the pecan tree and pulled up two good sized sweet potatoes. "Oh yeah, boy, these is good ones." She gathered all her baskets and took her bounty into the house, where Michel was brewing coffee and eating fresh peaches.

"Think I'll drive the cab a little while today," he announced. "Might have another good day. That taxidermist convention is still in town. They're going around all over town with stuffed birds and raccoons and such. Fella got in the cab yesterday with a stuffed buzzard that had Mardi Gras beads strung around it's neck. Ugliest thing I've ever seen, except maybe your cousin Josephine."

Eugenia set all her baskets on the table and began sorting vegetables. "Poor Josephine. She can't help it she's got all that hair on her face and one a' her ears is missing. She was born that way. She been going to the doctor for shots. The hairs is falling right off. She's been shaving the patches that's left. And she grew her hair longer so it covers her ears." Eugenia rinsed her vegetables in the sink and set them out on the drain. "Besides, she's not no uglier than your Uncle Armand."

"Well now, that's the sad truth, there," agreed Michel. "Uncle Armand has got to be the ugliest human being I've ever laid eyes on. Looks just like a big ole gorilla. I bet he's the reason that swamp

Just Off the Streetcar Line

monster story got started back in the fifties. Somebody saw Uncle Armand and thought it was Bigfoot."

Eugenia laughed and poured herself a cup of what her daughter had dubbed the worst coffee in Southeastern Louisiana. Eugenia said it wasn't bad, it just wasn't like that wimpy stuff that Nadine drank, that "capychena" stuff. "I'd say he's ugly because he's a hunnert an five, but he's been ugly ever since I can remember. Wonder what keeps him going?"

Michel laid his peach pits on the window sill to dry. "He says it's because he drinks swamp water, never got married and don't speak no English. I think it's probly 'cause he's too ornery to die."

"Maybe you ought to go down to the fishing camp today instead of drivin' the cab, look in on him. Take the can of bug spray with you. Them mosquitoes down there can carry off a small child."

Michel finished his coffee and set the cup in the sink. "You're probably right. Uncle Armand always says he can take care of himself, don't want nobody hovering over him. Sets his traps and his pots and all. But he's slowing down a little bit, arthritis you know. Think I'll go down by the camp this afternoon, take the pirogue out, check on my crab pots."

Eugenia rustled around in the pantry and started placing items in a plastic milk crate. "Here, you can take him this pound of coffee and a big jar of honey. Got some more stuff here he can have." By the time

Michel rinsed out his cup, the honey and coffee had company. Eugenia filled up the crate with jars of okra, tomatoes, corn relish, fig preserves, pickled peaches, sweet cucumber pickles, deer jerky and a big jar of plum wine. She topped it all off with a loaf of her homemade cinnamon bread, sealed in a plastic bag.

"Don't give him nothin' storebought," Michel told her. "You know he won't eat white people's food. Says the government puts something in storebought food that makes people go crazy and lose their hair."

Eugenia laughed. "He is one onery old Indian, that's for sure. I love his cantankerous old ass, though. He's a good man, is Uncle Armand."

Michel nodded. "Smart, too. Might be right about the food; you never know."

"I don't know about that, Michel. We both might be crazy, but we still got our hair."

*****

Avery Billiot woke with a start. He was slumped on his mother's sofa with the TV remote control in his hand. The sun was streaming through the lace curtains and some guy on the Shopping Network was demonstrating electric toilets. Avery reflected momentarily about the dangers of sitting on such a toilet during a thunderstorm, then turned off the TV and headed for the bathroom. Twenty-five minutes later his body was clean, his teeth were brushed and his face was shaven. Avery was physically ready to meet the world, but his spirit needed coffee. He started a pot brewing, then walked out the back door to say his morning prayers.

Avery stood in the middle of the pink flamingoes and assorted plastic wildlife. First he bowed to the east, then to the south, the west and the north. After paying homage to the four directions, he thanked the Creator for all his blessings. Then he thanked Mother Earth and Father Sky for getting him through one more night – especially last night – and for receiving him for one more day. Then he went back inside and made a tuna, cheese, onion, jalapeno and rice omelet to go with his sixty-four ounce tumbler of coffee.

His mother had awakened him around two o'clock, when Julia and Francis had shown up to babysit Miss Libby. Julia told him she could hear him snoring half way down the block. Avery's snoring was legendary. Once when he'd gone camping in Arkansas, another camper had alerted a park ranger because she thought there was a bear in the camp. Avery was very surprised to be awakened mid-snore by a frightened young and inexperienced forest ranger sticking a rifle through his tent flaps. Avery jumped up and grabbed the business end of the rifle, pulling in the ranger into the tent. The rifle went off and sent a bullet whizzing through Avery's tent and into the bathhouse thirty feet away, where the woman who called the forest ranger was cowering in her bathrobe. She ran screaming from the bathhouse, only to be confronted by a shaking Ranger Bill and a very naked, enraged Avery Billiot, who was complaining loudly about crazy white people with guns. The paranoid white lady decamped the next morning and Ranger Bill decided it was time to go back home to St. Paul, Minnesota and join his father in the hardware business. Avery continued his life pretty much as usual.

    Avery finished his meal, pushed his plate back and surveyed the big kitchen. Every available surface was covered with baked goods, and the refrigerator was loaded down with food. His mother had been cooking for a week, and tonight and tomorrow morning food would start arriving with the guests. Tonight relatives and friends would come to sleep on extra beds, couches and the floor, and Avery would put up his lodge in the big back yard and sleep there so his ninety-four-year-old grandmother could have his bed. Tomorrow night they would barbecue over a hundred pounds of meat, fish and poultry; there would be drumming and dancing and pipe smoking; and there would almost certainly be too much drinking. Tomorrow night the entire neighborhood plus about two hundred relatives and friends were invited to the wedding of Avery Red Hawk Billiot and Samantha Running Fox.

    Avery had been married once before, during his twenties, a marriage he referred to as his "most unfortunate incident". His former bride's name was Christina Chauvin, a white Catholic girl who was short on brains, personality and physical attributes. When asked by his family why he'd married her, Avery replied, "a bottle of Wild Turkey." After eight years, Avery sobered up and returned to traditional Indian ways, spending a lot of time in the bayou learning to become a *traittor* like his grandfather.

When Christina's light bulb finally went off and she realized that she was married to a real, live Indian who was following in the footsteps of his ancestors, she tried to have Avery committed on the grounds that he was "too Indian". Unfortunately for Christina, she tried to have the commitment papers signed by Judge Henri Dardard, Avery's uncle and fishing buddy. Judge Dardard not only refused to sign the commitment papers, he threatened to throw Christina in jail for violating Avery's civil rights. He also told her if she had one brain cell left in her ugly head she would stay out of his parish, where every other person was either a Dardard or a Billiot. Christina was dumb enough to call the judge an old gas bag and leave in a huff. The next morning she found an eight foot alligator with Mardi Gras beads around his neck chained to the bumper of her car. The Wildlife and Fisheries agent, one Louis Billiot, was very unsympathetic and refused to pick up the alligator. The police were similarly unhelpful. Christina finally convinced someone at the Audubon Zoo to take the reptile, which by now was attracting quite a crowd and had tried to eat her poodle, Muffy, who had foolishly gone outside to bark at it.

Avery, who had been at his mother's house during all the alligator commotion, arrived at his house about the time the zoo truck showed up. He was accompanied by his cousin, Deputy Sheriff Antoine Dardard, who helped him pack his belongings and clear out of the house. When Christina started screaming at Avery, Antoine shot a hole in the ceiling and told her to "shut the fuck up, bitch," whereupon she locked herself in the bathroom. When she emerged approximately two hours later, Avery and Antoine were gone and Muffy was dangling from the ceiling fan in the dining room by her little tail, slowing revolving and throwing up her breakfast.

Since his divorce fifteen years earlier, Avery had lived with several young women – including one who was barely voting age and another one who sported seven tattoos and a navel ring – but he had shied away from marriage, not wanting to repeat his "most unfortunate incident". But now he was forty-five years old and he had found Samantha, the woman of his dreams, and he was tying the knot once more.

Samantha Running Fox was forty-three, pretty and smart, a successful Native American artist who sold her paintings all over the United States and Canada. Her first husband had announced on their tenth wedding anniversary that he had fallen in love with a man named Leonard; her second husband had left her after five years of marriage to live with two lesbians – he claimed he was in love with both of them. She had naturally been a little gun-shy of marriage ever since. Avery assured Samantha that he had no such kinky leanings, and promised her that she could hang him by his dick from the ceiling if he ever expressed such desires. She said she'd hold him to that.

    Avery had met Samantha at the folk life booth the first weekend of Jazz Fest, where he was selling his crafts and she was selling her paintings. By the second weekend of Jazz Fest he had convinced her to marry him. While they were sitting in the rain listening to Dr. John sing a song about Humpty Dumpty, Avery told Samantha she was the girl for him, he'd never love anybody else, and they really ought to get married right away before they lost their nerve. He said he wasn't a psycho serial killer or a closet transvestite. He said he had never hit a woman, didn't drink or do drugs, and he had never lusted after another man, but he wasn't sure he'd never lusted after a lesbian. He was just a straight-up normal guy and she could come home with him and meet his mama and all his relatives, they'd vouch for him. He said his ex-wife had tried to have him committed for being an Indian and one of his girlfriends said he was a sex maniac because he wanted to get laid more than once every two weeks, but other than that he couldn't think of anybody who thought he was especially weird, except that girl he'd run off at a pow wow once when he offered to make her an Indian by injection. Samantha laughed and said that was the best pickup line she'd ever heard. She told him if he'd live up to his reputation as a sex maniac, she'd marry him. He promised to try. That was three weeks ago and she hadn't complained yet.

Tomorrow night Avery and Samantha would be married in front of their friends and most of his relatives. He'd said he wanted to meet her family, but she said most of them were dead. She said her brother Luther was still alive but he'd gone nuts and joined a cult (the Baptists); they hadn't spoken since he'd called her from North Carolina to tell her he'd found God. She told him she didn't realize God had been lost and Luther hung up on her. Samantha said she had a sister, Ruby, but she was crazy, too; she just never had been the same since that botched boob job left her lopsided, and then her husband ran off with a topless mud wrestler.

Samantha hadn't spoken to her sister since they had shared an apartment in Miami and Ruby accused her of stealing her glow-in-the-dark condoms. Samantha told Ruby she'd used them herself when she got drunk and took home that male stripper from the Trap Door Club, but Ruby became so unreasonable that Samantha decided her life was much more peaceful without Ruby in it, moved out the next day, and hadn't spoken to Ruby in over five years. When Avery said glow-in-the-dark condoms was a pretty strange reason for not speaking for five years, Samantha sighed and said, well Ruby also believed that aliens had planted transmitters in her head, and she claimed to have had sex with Bigfoot in the Redwood Forest. She also swore she was in contact with Elvis, who wasn't really dead but was living on a boat in the Bahamas. While these stories made life interesting, and alone were certainly no reason to stop speaking to her sister,

Samantha said Ruby also carried a gun, which was nothing strange since she lived in Miami, but she regularly took potshots at car tires (she particularly hated rental cars) and streetlights. Life with Ruby was just too dangerous. Avery asked what Ruby's problem was, and Samantha replied, "Drinking mostly, along with PMS, pantyhose, the wrong men. The same things that make most women crazy."

*****

Miss Libby was in her backyard digging a hole, wearing a diaphanous pale green nightgown over her hot pink bra and panties, along with a pair of bright yellow rainboots. At seventy-three, with her bright orange hair and one hundred eighty pounds sitting on her five foot two inch frame, she was a sight to behold. When the hole was big enough, she gently placed the remains of her weed eater in the bottom and covered it with dirt. It had been a good friend; now it was gone to appliance heaven and Miss Libby just didn't know what she was going to do with herself.

Julia and Francis had left at four-thirty that morning, after Miss Libby promised to never touch another motorized gardening tool again as long as she lived. They threatened to put her in a home, then they threatened to take her to live with one of them, but the truth was, neither of them wanted to live with their mother and neither of them could afford to send her to live in an assisted care apartment. Besides, they both knew that Miss Libby would just cause trouble wherever she went. They did tell her, however, if she didn't straighten up that they would hire a companion for her, which was a lot cheaper than an assisted care facility. Since Miss Libby found all the aforementioned options objectionable, she promised to behave and her children left before dawn.

Miss Libby knew that her children did not want her living with them, and she certainly did not want to live with either of them. Julia was married to an airplane mechanic and had three teenage children. She had her hands absolutely full with soccer, slumber parties, pool parties, music recitals, and noisy family life in general. Francis, on the other hand, had never married and was currently living in the lower Garden District with a bartender named Ivan and a Siberian Husky named Rasputin. Miss Libby loved her children and her grandchildren, but they drove her nuts, especially those teenagers, who played loud music and talked on the phone all the time. She preferred to be left alone in her own home that had been paid off for the last twenty-one years.

Miss Libby patted down the rest of the dirt, leaned on the shovel and sighed. What was she going to do now? She didn't enjoy crafts or sewing or cooking. Learning to knit at the senior center was absolute torture; she was just terrible at it and all she'd made was a scarf that looked so bad she'd given it to Eugenia's cats. She watched the soaps during the day, but nights were lonely and now she had nothing left to look forward to except the gardening shows. Topiary art had been her life. She took the shovel back to the shed and looked over in the corner at the hedging shears. Miss Libby brightened up immediately. She'd been using the weed whacker for so long she'd forgotten about the shears. She had promised her children she would never touch another motorized garden tool, but she hadn't said a word about *manual* tools.

*****

Marsha Fellows woke up at nine-thirty, groggy and achy from a drug induced sleep. Marsha always took sleeping pills that knocked her out cold for at least ten hours. She looked over at Graham's bed – they had been sleeping in twin beds for the last eighteen years. As usual, Graham had come in late and left early. He always made his bed before he left, and he never stayed to have breakfast with Marsha. He told her he usually met with students or other faculty for breakfast, or just sat alone to read the paper and drink his coffee. (In truth, of course, he usually had breakfast with Isabella somewhere in the Quarter, and hadn't spent one minute of the night in the twin bed uptown.) Marsha slowly pulled herself out of bed and contemplated the day ahead of her.

Marsha had not worked since the second year of her marriage, when she and Graham had moved from Philadelphia to New Hampshire. Even when she had worked, she had not enjoyed it. Her degree in Medieval Studies had prepared her for absolutely nothing, and she wasn't trained in anything practical. She could not type or even work a copy machine properly. She had gotten a job in a bookstore, but she couldn't get the hang of the cash register, so she was fired. She got a job as a sales clerk in a clothing store, but her sour disposition turned away customers, so she was fired again. She tried working as a teacher's assistant in a private kindergarten, but she was fired for screaming at the children. She then tried working in a candy factory, but was fired for being too slow. Her last job was waitressing at a diner, where she was fired after dumping spaghetti into a customer's lap. Graham had suggested she learn to be a beautician or a decorator or *something*, but then they had moved up to Dartmouth and there were no opportunities for her to do much of anything except be a professor's wife.

In reality, Marsha was lazy. She was rather plain in appearance, terribly insecure and not the brightest bulb in the chandelier. All she really wanted to do since arriving in Louisiana was read romance novels and watch soap operas. When she and Graham had lived in New England, she had ridden her bicycle a lot and taken long walks, but it was too hot and humid in New Orleans at least six months out of the year to ride or walk, and most of the streets were unfit for biking. Marsha was certain that New Orleans was the pothole capital of the United States. She also had no friends in Louisiana at all. At Dartmouth she'd had a couple of friends of long duration who were, like her, unhappy wives of professors. She also had a secret relationship.

Just Off the Streetcar Line

After the move to New Hampshire, Graham traveled a great deal, usually without Marsha, and even when he was at home, he ignored her most of the time. After too many years of this lonely, unfulfilling life, Marsha befriended a professor of anthropology, Edwina Holmes. Edwina was beautiful in a masculine sort of way: tall and muscular, small ass and big tits, dark red hair cut very short, creamy white skin. She always wore pants, occasionally smoked cigars, drank scotch. And she could do anything a man could do: chop wood, fix a car, roof a house, shoot game. Marsha admired her enormously and began to seek out her company not long after they'd met at a faculty party one Labor Day weekend. On a fine fall day in October, Edwina took Marsha out to her cabin in the woods, where she spent most of her weekends. After a long hike, Edwina stripped off all her clothes in front of the fireplace in the living room and asked Marsha to join her for a shower. That was the beginning of a relationship that was still on-going.

The years in New England with Edwina were the happiest years of Marsha's life. Edwina had awakened something in her that no man ever had. Of course, Marsha had only had sex with three men in her life, none of it very satisfactory. She had never really been interested in having sex with men, she just used it as a tool for trapping a man into marriage, which for some strange reason she thought would make her happy.

The first time Marsha had sex she was sixteen, when she made it in the back seat of a 1960 Buick with a boy named Jerry. After three repeat performances, she suggested they get married and Jerry suggested she was out of her everlovin' mind. When he got out of the car to take a leak, Marsha set the back seat on fire. Needless to say, they never had another date. She didn't have the nerve to try sex again until her sophomore year of college. Her second lover was a good looking guy from her English Lit class, Paul Larosa. After six months of perfunctory sex with Paul, he announced that he was leaving school to marry a freshman he'd gotten pregnant. Marsha did not take this news well. She screamed and cried and trashed his apartment. She also damn near killed him with a heavy ashtray that luckily only grazed his skull. And she threatened to blow up his car. Paul backhanded her and pushed her out the door into the hallway, where she kicked the door and screamed obscenities until someone called the police.

A year after the Paul Larosa disaster, Marsha started dating Graham. As graduation neared and Graham had given no indication that he was contemplating matrimony, Marsha staged a phony pregnancy that trapped Graham into marrying her. It had not been a happy union and Graham had threatened to leave her many times. He eventually stopped threatening to leave and just ignored her most of the time, traveling without her every chance he got. They made a pretense of marriage for appearances, but it was very strained. They only had sex when Graham got very, very drunk, which meant he usually passed out pretty fast, and they hadn't had sex at all since they'd moved south a year ago, which was fine with Marsha.

She had no interest in Graham, who obviously had no interest in her either.

Marsha wasn't very bright, but she wasn't completely stupid either. She knew Graham had affairs – she'd found some photographs he tried to explain away but she didn't believe him. Since she'd met Edwina, though, she really didn't care what Graham was doing. She was leaving him anyway. Since Marsha's move to Louisiana, she had flown to Boston twice to see Edwina, and Edwina had traveled to New Orleans on three different occasions. The last time had been a few weeks ago, during the first weekend of Jazz Fest. Graham had gone off to some conference in San Francisco for a week, and Marsha had spent four days with Edwina at the Hotel Intercontinental. They had gone to the Jazz Fest, which Marsha hated, but she put up with the crowds and the heat and the dirt and the loud, obnoxious people because she loved Edwina, who loved festivals. At the end of the trip, Edwina begged her to move back to New England and live with her, and Marsha promised to do so by the end of May. Unbeknownst to Graham, most of Marsha's clothing and personal things had already been shipped to Edwina's, and Marsha had cleaned out their joint savings account, which only amounted to twenty-six thousand dollars. She was planning to pack up everything else over the weekend and drive out of New Orleans on Monday morning. She was leaving Graham lock, stock and furniture. He could have everything. She just wanted Edwina.

*****

Lucille was attempting to free her cat's head from the vacuum cleaner tube when the phone rang.

"Are you doing anything important?" asked Leola.

"Just pulling Telemachus' head out of the Electralux tube. Hold on." She grabbed the wriggling cat with both hands and stepped on the tube, then pulled with all her might. Telemachus dug his claws into the rug and growled, but his head popped free and he jumped up on top of the sideboard to clean himself. Lucille picked up the phone. "Okay. He'll live."

"How'd he get his head stuck in there?"

"Who knows. He must've been playing with something interesting. I hope I didn't suck up a dead mouse."

"Better to suck up a dead mouse than a live one. Come on over. I made breakfast."

Lucille hung up and walked the ten feet from her back door to Leola's. "Your cannas are blooming," she announced, grabbing a plate from the dish drain.

Leola was pouring coffee. "Aren't they pretty? They look just like red silk."

They sat down at the red and white enamel table and started filling their plates. "You must've been hungry this morning," observed Lucille. "You cooked enough for six people."

"It'll keep. I didn't eat much dinner. I was working on that quilt for Marjory and forgot to eat. By the time I remembered I hadn't eaten, it was late, so I just ate some leftover chicken livers."

"They give me heartburn."

"Everything gives you heartburn."

"That's why I drink Barq's."

They turned their attention to the jalapeno corn fritters, smothered pork chops, crawfish dressing and beignets. When Leola came up for air, she raised one eyebrow and said, "Guess who I saw coming out the back of the Cheramie house late last night?"

"Michael Flaherty. I saw him, too, the little stinker."

"Wonder how he explains his late hours to that sweet little Melanie? And her pregnant! I don't know what is wrong with that boy."

Lucille shrugged her shoulders. "Lots of men can't keep their drawers on. Look at Vinnie."

Leola nodded her head. "And look where it landed him – right in the river. I just hope Michael comes to his senses before he winds up face down somewhere."

"Melanie would never hurt a fly. It'd break her little heart, though."

Leola grabbed another fritter. "Wasn't talking about Melanie. I was thinking about her daddy."

Lucille's forkful of dressing halted midway to her mouth. "They never did prove he killed Lionel Traina."

"Maybe not, but sure as I'm sitting here, Bennie Lanassa shot Lionel in the head, then cut off his penis and stuck it up his ass."

"Oh, I'm sure he *did* it, I just said they never did *prove* it." Lucille stuffed the last corner of a beignet in her mouth. "I wonder why he left Lionel stark naked wearing nothing but his cowboy boots, though. Left him hanging from the jungle gym in Audubon Park. Nobody saw anything, of course."

Leola got up to pour more coffee. "Don't you remember? That's what Lionel was wearing when Bennie came home and found him with his wife. When Bennie came in the back door, Lionel grabbed his shirt and ran out the front door, but he dropped the shirt on the ground. He jumped in his car wearing nothing but the cowboy boots. I guess Bennie didn't kill him then and there because he never could've gotten away with it."

"Obviously he couldn't catch him, either," said Lucille. "He was moving pretty fast. I thought what Bennie did to Vera was pretty tacky."

"A married woman screwing a siding salesman in her own kitchen in the middle of the day is pretty tacky, too."

"Not as tacky as Bennie duct taping her naked to the top of the car with a carrot sticking out of her butt. Gloria Bourgeois said she nearly fainted when she came home and saw Vera over there next door taped to the car; she thought she was dead. She pulled the carrot out of her butt, cut off the tape and took her inside and called the police. I'm glad little Melanie was away at camp when that happened."

"It must have been mortifying for the poor little thing when Bennie was arrested on suspicion of murder, even though it never even went to trial. No weapon, no witnesses, no evidence."

Lucille put the dishes in the sink and Leola started wrapping up food and sticking it in the refrigerator. "Whatever happened to Vera?" asked Lucille.

"Don't you remember? She had Bennie arrested for beating her with a wooden spoon and sodomizing her with the carrot. She said he pulled the spoon right out of the cake mix, pushed her down on the kitchen table and started whacking her with the spoon, then taped her to the car. Gloria said she had chocolate cake mix and bruises all over her butt."

Lucille said, "I remember all that. I just wondered whatever happened to her since."

Leola pulled two cokes out of the refrigerator and handed one to Lucille. "She cleaned out their joint account the next morning while Bennie was in jail and left town. Gina Thibodeaux told her mother – you know Lydia Thibodeaux who works over at Walgreen's – she told her that Melanie said her mother was living in Brazil. Guess she figured Bennie wouldn't go all the way to South America to kill her."

They headed for the front room. "Wonder what she's doing in Brazil," Lucille said.

"Melanie told Gina that Vera's the top salesperson for a manufacturer of feminine protection products."

Lucille stared at Leola for approximately ten seconds. "You mean like Kotex?"

"Exactly."

"Well, there's money in that, I'm sure. I'd just hate for my business card to read 'Kotex Salesman'. It's embarrassing."

"Not half as embarrassing as being taped to a car with a carrot stuck up your butt."

Lucille giggled. "Like an X-rated Bugs Bunny!"

"Lucille, you're bad!"

They settled on the couch and turned on the TV. It was time for "All My Children".

*****

Jimmy Jackson's phone rang just as he was headed for lunch. It was his grandmother. "Jimmy, I got to go to Dillard's tonight."

Jimmy sighed inwardly. He was taking Alice to dinner at seven. "What for, Grandmamma?"

"For a wedding present for Avery. You didn't forget about the wedding tomorrow night did you?"

"No ma'am, I didn't forget."

"Is Alice coming?"

"Yes ma'am, she's coming. She's already bought a gift. It can be from all of us."

"No siree, it cannot. I'll pick out my own gift, thank you, but I got to go to Dillard's."

Jimmy looked at his watch. "Okay, Grandmamma. Why don't I leave work early, like around three, and take you to Dillard's? You have anything particular in mind you want to buy?"

"Bath towels. Everybody needs bath towels. I'd get sheets, but I don't know what size bed they gonna have. He's out there right now puttin' up that tipi in the back yard. I can see him from here. I wonder if they're planning on living out there."

"Who's putting up a tipi?"

Grandmamma snorted at his ignorance. "Well Avery, of course. Who else do you know who would be puttin' up a tipi in his mama's back yard? I guess they gonna be drinkin' over there tomorrow night. When they start drinkin', you take me home, Jimmy. I don't wanna be 'round no drinkin'."

"Yes ma'am."

"I know Avery don't drink no more, but some a' his kin drink like there's no tomorrow. They get all liquored up and start drummin' and singin' them songs about loose women, and then they all pass out in the yard. Last year they didn't wake up 'til Larry's dogs went over there and peed on some of 'em. They thought it was raining and they all staggered in the house. Livonia ran 'em all back outside and turned the hose on 'em. It was disgusting."

Jimmy stiffled a laugh. He actually thought it was funny as hell, but he couldn't let his grandmother know that. "Grandmamma, I have to go. I'm meeting the mayor for lunch."

"Well I got a thing or two to tell His Honor." Oh lord, Jimmy groaned inwardly. "I'd like to know when that pothole in front of the house is gonna be fixed. It's big enough to swim in. And when is he gonna do something about all these chillens ridin' around in their cars with the stereo up so loud it sounds like thunder? Boom-etty-boom-etty-boom-boom! Sounds like a earthquake."

"Grandmamma, I don't think the mayor can do anything about –"

"Now you listen to me. He's the mayor. He can do somethin' about it if he wants to. Did you give him my letters?"

Hell no. "Yes ma'am, I sent them over there."

"Well I never heard nothin' back from him. And furthermore, that den of iniquity down the street –"

"What den of iniquity?"

"That Suds and Buds place where all the old mens washes they clothes and gets drunk. It's just fulla hussy women parading around flashing themselves, tempting old men with the devil. Gawd only knows what goes on in that place."

As far as Jimmy knew, the most interesting thing that had ever happened at the Suds and Buds was when Leroy Jefferson and Vernon Dunbar got into a fight about the LSU Tigers and Vernon put Leroy's little chihuahua in the spin cycle. Poor little Pedro couldn't walk straight for half an hour. Vernon and Leroy stood on opposite street corners yelling things like, "Come on over here, fool, so's I can punch yo' ugly face," and making swinging motions. This went on for fifteen or twenty minutes, until Wilma Jefferson appeared and wanted to know where the hell her laundry was, she couldn't go to preachin' in dirty drawers, and what in God's name was wrong with her little Pedro, did you all get him drunk again?

"Grandmamma, I'll speak to the mayor about that, and I'll pick you up about three-thirty. I'll take you shopping."

Grandmamma, who had obviously run out of steam, just said, "You my angel, Jimmy. I love you sweet boy."

"I love you, too, Grandmamma."

*****

Dave Richard sat on a barstool at the Suds and Buds, drinking a cold Turbo Dog and watching "The Young and the Restless" with his fellow stool-sitters while his clothing slowly tossed in the big dryer behind him. It was a quiet afternoon, with only an occasional outburst from either Luther Celestine or Kenny

Livaudais, both regular patrons of Suds and Buds and obviously loyal soap opera fans.

Luther snorted and threw a pretzel at the TV screen. "Who do you think you foolin', bitch? You no good for him, just a little snake in the grass."

Kenny nodded in agreement. "She just a hussy, tha's all. Not like that purty little blonde girl on "General Hospital", the one that's got tuberculosis."

"Ain't tuberculosis, it's a brain tumor, dimwit," argued Luther. "That little blonde babe on "All My Children" got tuberculosis."

Kenny's head jerked around about the same time he tried to take another sip of Bud, managing to miss his mouth and pour beer down his neck. "Kelly Ripa's got tuberculosis?!"

"No, you fool, not Kelly Ripa, the other blonde, the real skinny one with big knockers."

Dave was trying desperately to keep up with this stimulating conversation, but he was not a regular soap watcher and was hopelessly lost. Dave did not normally sit around in the middle of the day, drinking Turbo Dog at the Suds and Buds and watching soap operas, but his washing machine at home was currently possessed. He had gone home for lunch and decided to put a load of laundry in the washer, since the hamper was overflowing. He was polishing off half a muffuletta when he heard a horrible thumping and clanging coming from the laundry room. He ran into the room just as the lid flew off the washing machine and his dripping, soapy clothing flew around the room like big, wet pelicans. There was soap everywhere — on the ceiling, the window, the floor and the walls, and on Dave, who'd been hit by a flying pair of bluejeans in the fracas. The washer belched smoke and hissed, then died with a groan. Dave knew that whatever kind of mechanical gris-gris was at work here, it was beyond his expertise to fix it, so he gathered his sopping wet clothes, wrapped them in an old shower curtain and threw them in the brand new garbage can that he had not even dragged to the curb yet, and rolled his load down the street to the Suds and Buds. He felt kind of stupid rolling his garbage can full of wet clothes down the street, but no once gave him or his trashcan a second glance.

Dave was loading one of the washers when Delia Devereaux arrived with her laundry packed in a shopping cart she'd borrowed from the A&P fourteen years ago, when her kids were little. Delia had six different children by four different men, two of them ex-husbands, the other two best forgotten. She lived in a converted double with her mother, grandmother, aunt and brother, and of course the younger children. Delia's grandmother sat on the porch and had long conversations with her dead husband; her mother wouldn't leave the house because, she said, there were aliens who could get her if she went outside — she swore they were scaly and green and lived in the shed out back. Her aunt cooked all the time and sang hymns, talked about Jesus and "going to glory." She was such a pain in the ass about Jesus, even the Jehovah's Witnesses avoided her. Delia's brother Tom was a Vietnam vet who suffered from post-traumatic stress syndrome. He mostly sat on the front steps looking at old copies of *Playboy*, muttering "you fine baby" to himself, and shooting at imaginary VC with his nephew's super-soaker water rifle. The neighbors occasionally got wet, but Tom was a harmless soul. For some years Delia worked as a meter maid for the city but finally couldn't take the stress any longer and quit. Besides, Delia wasn't mean enough to be a New Orleans meter maid — she just didn't have that pit bull personality required for the job. Now she delivered pizzas at night for Papa John's and was much happier. The tips were good and her family always had plenty of pizza. Dave looked at Delia and thought about her family and silently counted his blessings.

*****

Louie was standing in his kitchen wearing nothing but his Mickey Mouse jockey shorts, making a tuna po'boy. He heaped the contents of the deli carton onto French bread, then dressed it with lettuce and tomatoes. The tuna salad from Lorio's contained everything but the kitchen sink: tuna, eggs, apples, raisins, walnuts, grapes, sweet relish, jalapenos, black olives, grilled onions, Cajun mustard and mayonnaise. Louie rarely cooked for himself; he lived on carryout from Popeye's, Papa John's Pizza and other local restaurants and delis. Occasionally his girlfriend-of-the-month cooked for him, but his relationships were generally very short-lived; none of his women hung around long enough for him to get used to home cooking. Not that he'd ever had the opportunity to grow accustomed to home cooking anyway.

When Louie was growing up, his family went through a long procession of cooks and maids. The cooks were an international group, spanning the ethnic globe. In the twenty-two years he had lived in his parents house on State Street, his mother, Vivienne, who could not boil eggs properly, had gone through a series of cooks from Thailand, Nicaragua, Haiti, Columbia, Cuba, India, Greece, the Philippines, France, Italy, Mexico, Texas and New Orleans. His mother had not run off any of the cooks – she was a lovable, if somewhat spacey woman – she had just had bad luck. The girls from Thailand and India both left to get married; the Nicaraguan and the Mexican were illegal aliens. The Haitian grew controlled substances in the garden and occasionally spiked the food with his special herbs, creating truly memorable evenings, like the time his mother couldn't find her car after dinner. It was in the driveway, but she was too stoned to find the driveway *or* the car. She finally sat down in the front yard and sang the Star Spangled Banner until Louie's father took her inside and put her to bed. The French and Italian cooks were living in the U.S. on limited visas they couldn't renew, so they each lasted a year. The Greek was a drunk who sautéed the goldfish from the backyard pond; the Cuban not only had a drinking problem but also practiced Santeria (he got loaded one night and tried to sacrifice Louie's collie, who bit him on the ass and chased him up a crepe myrtle); the Columbian was deported on drug charges. The girl from Manila attempted to execute the Siamese cat, which she had planned to put in the stewpot. The little sexpot from Texas was dismissed after Mrs. Bourgeois caught her and Mr. Bourgeois getting it on in Louie's old treehouse when Louie was fourteen. Louie wasn't the least bit surprised when it happened; he had been spying on his old man and an impressive cadre of nubile lovelies since he was eight. He always said it was good training for his future vocation. The only cook who lasted for any length of time was Elmera, who was a two hundred fifty pound black woman from the lower Ninth Ward who was such a good cook his father declared he would give up sex if she would stay with them forever. Elmera told him she didn't care what he did with his doohickey so long as she got paid. She was still there after thirty years. Louie didn't know if his father actually gave up sex, but he seriously doubted it.

Louie sat down at the kitchen table, consuming his enormous po'boy and thinking about his own illicit sexual activity earlier that morning. Making love to Betty had been a delightful diversion, but he knew better than to see her again. He generally steered clear of married women. Married women had husbands, children, other married friends – everything he didn't need to complicate his life.

Louie tended to date young, unattached waitresses, with a few forays into other professional pools. For seven months once he had dated a beautiful cop named Felicia who was only a few years younger than him, but she really wanted to get married and have children, so they broke up and Louie went back to dating twenty-five-year-old waitresses he met at bars like Later Gator and The Sleeping Dog.

Louie was pulling a tee-shirt over his head when he heard a soft knock at his side door. He checked his watch; Millie Devereaux was five minutes early. She had called yesterday and made an appointment but hadn't specified what type of snooping she wanted him to do. He assumed she wanted him to spy on her husband, because that was ninety percent of his business, but for all he knew she was looking for a lost cat. He occasionally got an insurance case, which usually involved taking pictures of some poor slob with or without his crutches/neck brace/jockey cup and was about as much fun as watching paint dry. He wished just once he would get a Nero Wolf type case involving exceptionally civilized murder and/or mayhem, with a beautiful femme fatale thrown in for good measure. He sighed. This was real life; murder and mayhem were never civilized, and beautiful femmes fatale were in short supply. He opened the side door and promptly fell in lust with the little blonde angel in a miniskirt standing on his porch.

He didn't know if Millie was a femme fatale, but she certainly was beautiful: heart shaped face, big blue eyes, masses of pale blonde curls cascading over her shoulders. No wedding ring. He took her to his office, settled her in the red leather chair, and asked her what he could do to help her. He tried very hard not to look at her absolutely astounding legs.

Millie fished around in her shoulder bag, then handed him a photograph of a handsome blonde man standing next to a cute little redhead on what appeared to be a small yacht. "I want you to run a check on this guy, follow him, find out everything about him that you can."

Louie studied the photo. "Who is he?"

"Danny Darrow. His home and office addresses are on the back." Louie flipped over the picture and noted addresses for an apartment on upper Prytania Street and an office downtown in the warehouse district.

"Why do you want him investigated?"

Millie scowled. "He's trying to get himself engaged to my sister Veronica. I don't trust him."

"Does Veronica live here?"

"Across the lake. Mandeville."

Louie caught himself staring at Millie's thighs and mentally undressing her. He cleared his throat and wrote down "Veronica - Mandeville". "Uh, why don't you trust Mr. Darrow?"

"He's too slick, says things that don't add up. Very secretive about his business – says he's an entrepreneur, but he's vague on the details. And he comes on to me all the time."

I don't blame him, thought Louie. "What does he say that doesn't add up?"

"He doesn't know where Little Italy is."

Louie blinked at his prospective client. "So?"

"He says he's from New York, but he doesn't know where Little Italy is. He tried to bluff me, but he doesn't know where it is. And he calls Sixth Avenue "Avenue of the Americas". If he were really from New York, he wouldn't. Other little things, too."

Louie wrote "New York" on a legal pad. "Like what?"

"Like he says he's from a rich family, but he has the table manners of a rhinoceros. His accent is wrong, too; he sounds more like he's from the midwest then New York. And maybe a hint of some other accent, too, but I can't identify it. And he says he went to Columbia University, but when he started describing it, I realized he was talking about NYU."

Louie scribbled "midwest - NYU - Columbia - rhino" on his pad. "That would be pretty easy to verify. I take it you've spent some time in New York."

Millie nodded her beautiful blonde head. "I'm up there all the time. My older sister Madeleine lives there. She owns a reptile house in the East Village."

"Reptile house?"

"You know, snakes, lizards, chameleons. She got interested in them when we were living in Belize in the early eighties. She sleeps with an iguana."

Interesting family, thought Louie. He leaned back in his chair. "So why would this guy try to snow-job your sister? Unless he's just a compulsive liar, of course."

"I think he's a fortune hunter. You see, our parents left us quite a lot of money. They were killed four years ago. Well, eaten actually."

Louie stared at her for a moment. *"Eaten?"*

"By crocodiles in the Amazon River. They fell out of the boat and were eaten. All the local guides ever found were a few body parts – my father's foot, my mother's left hand."

Louie was mesmerized. "God, I'm sorry. Jesus. What were they doing down there?"

"They were anthropologists. They were searching for a lost tribe of Indians in the rain forest. Blue pygmies."

"There are blue pygmies in the Amazon rain forest?"

"Well, they're not *really* blue; they *paint* themselves blue."

"Did they ever find them, the pygmies?"

"No, they didn't."

For no reason at all, Louie wrote "Blue Pygmies - Amazon" on his note pad. "Are you an anthropologist, too?"

Millie shook her head. "No, but I used to be an archaeologist. Now I'm a freelance writer. I submit articles to magazines like *National Geographic*, *Sierra Club*, *Arizona Highways*. Whoever will publish them. I like writing about the environment."

"What made you give up archaeology?"

Millie made a face. "The digs. You're always dirty, there's never any indoor plumbing, the food usually sucks, and you're always off in some primitive place, dealing with foreign governments and weird taboos. At twenty-five, it was an adventure. At thirty, it wasn't fun anymore. I got tired of eating grub worms and wiping myself with banana leaves. Besides, I'm a lesbian. Do you know how hard it is to find girlfriends on digs?" Louie felt his dick shrink as he shook his head. "Well, they're few and far between, let me tell you."

Louie sat up straight and cleared his throat. "About your sister...."

"Veronica."

"Veronica. Yes, well, I assume you want me to find out all I can about her unsuitable boyfriend."

"Absolutely everything. Check computer records, follow him, take pictures. Whatever. I want enough evidence to convince my sister that the little dork is a golddigger."

Millie gave him a retainer for two thousand dollars. He noted a French Quarter address and phone number on her check. As he watched her walk down the sidewalk toward her car, he shook his head sadly. The woman of his dreams was gay. It was the story of his life.

*****

Donnie Lee woke up on his sofa, stark naked except for the long red wig covering his crotch. His gold lame gown was draped over the hamster cage; Linus was munching on the sequins dangling through the little bars. For some reason his shoes were hanging by their stiletto heels from the brass light fixture and his brassiere was suspended from the ponytail palm in the corner of the room. Donnie got up and wandered around the living room, looking for any other missing items. He caught sight of something floating in the aquarium and, upon closer inspection, discovered the angel fish swimming in and out of the legs of his lacy underpants.

Donnie stumbled into the bathroom and stared at himself in the mirror and gasped. What the hell was that? It looked like big black spiders clinging to his forehead. When they didn't move, he slowly reached up and pulled his fake eyelashes from just under his hairline. They had traveled a few inches north in his sleep. Standing under a warm shower, Donnie marveled at his absence of hangover. True, he felt like the victim of a hit-and-run, but he had no headache whatsoever. He also had no memory past eleven o'clock last night. The diamond tennis bracelet was still secured to his wrist; it flashed and sparkled in the warm spray. Donnie emerged slowly from the shower, pink and rosey, wrapped himself in a big salmon-colored silk dressing gown he'd ordered from Victoria's Secret, and shuffled into his black and turquoise kitchen.

When Donnie's father died in a train wreck twenty years earlier, Donnie and his mother had used some of the considerable insurance and settlement money to completely renovate and redecorate the house. The result was something akin to the Jetsons meet Noel Coward, but it was quite colorful and suited Donnie Lee's personality to a tee. His own bedroom was straight out of a Jean Harlow movie, all satin and glamour.

Donnie Lee drank a weak Bloody Mary and consumed a jar of artichoke hearts, a bowl of jambalaya, and shrimp mousse heaped on Ritz crackers. His hunger sated, he wandered through the house, trying to decide what to do with the rest of his day.

Donnie Lee did not have to work. The $4.2 million settlement due to his father's untimely death was enough to keep him in evening gowns and feathered boas for the rest of his life. Donnie had a degree in Art History from LSU, but aside from working in a few art galleries when he was younger – plus six months at a health food store and that disastrous two-day stint at a kite shop where he managed to hang himself by the foot – he had never really worked. For the balance of his adult years, Donnie had stayed at home and taken care of his beloved mother. And taking care of Mama had been no irksome task. Mama was fun.

Mrs. Bergeron loved bingo parlors and casinos, and she was a great traveling companion. She and Donnie Lee had taken many trips together over the years: Las Vegas, Lake Tahoe, the Caribbean, Europe. Mama, a devout Catholic who loved to eat, had been particularly fond of Italy; they made five trips to Italy in ten years. Donnie swore she went there just to eat. The one place she refused to go was Germany. She was still mad about World War II and adamantly refused to set foot on German soil. She told Donnie not to be fooled by prevailing politics; leopards don't change their spots. She made her only son promise on her future grave that he would never go to Germany, and he had kept his promise. He had, however, gone to Austria nine months after her death and thoroughly enjoyed his time there.

After his mother's unfortunate death by gerbil, Donnie Lee had considered (a) buying a mansion or at least a condo in the Quarter, (b) taking a cruise around the world or at least as far as Cancun, or (c) moving to San Francisco. Upon further consideration, however, Donnie (a) could not bear to leave the house he had lived in his whole life, (b) got seasick in a ski boat on the Tangipahoa River, and (c) could never spend more than three weeks away from New Orleans before becoming hopelessly homesick, much less move three thousand miles away. Besides, he was afraid of earthquakes. So he remained in the house of his birth, visited places accessible by air, rail or interstate (but never for more than two or three weeks), and spent a great deal of time partying in the Quarter. And now that Mama was gone, he splurged on a sporty little BMW convertible. Red. (Mama only drove green Buicks and was almost certainly rolling in her grave over Donnie's choice of color and Bavarian engineering.)

Donnie Lee got out his daily "to do" list that he carried with him everywhere because he had a short-term memory like a sieve. He glanced over at his Mickey Mouse phone and wrote down "buy new cell phone" at the top of the page. His old cell phone had met with an unfortunate accident on Mardi Gras Day. He had been celebrating with the boys, watching the Rex parade on the Avenue and drinking pina coladas at ten o'clock in the morning, when nature called. He didn't think he could make it through the crowd all the way down the street to his friend Bunny's house, so he popped into one of the port-o-potties at the corner to relieve himself. Just as he was bending over, the phone slipped right out of his pocket and fell into the hole with a sad little plop and started to ring at that moment. Horrified, Donnie Lee stared into the black hole, then zipped up his pants, muttered "no way in hell," and left the port-o-potty with the phone still ringing. He forgot all about his phone until two days later, when he was sitting outside Copeland's with his friend Lola, eating shrimp and drinking a Cosmo. Just about the time he noticed that the port-o-potties had been mounted onto a big flatbed truck, a drunk with a bodily need climbed up on the truck and entered one of the potties. About a minute later, the driver jumped into the cab of the truck and started pulling out into the street. From somewhere deep inside one of the potties, Donnie heard it – the sound of a phone ringing. The drunk came lurching out of the potty hollering, "Hey! I'm in here! Hey, stop! Lemme out!" The truck driver stopped in the middle of the street and looked back at the drunk holding onto his pants. "Thanks man, I got to get off here." He lowered himself onto the street, then looked back at the driver and said, "Hey, you know the phone's ringin'." It was then that Donnie Lee realized that it was *his* phone ringing. And he wasn't about to claim it.

Donnie couldn't think of anything else to add to his list, so he retired to the living room to watch his favorite soaps. An hour later he was sprawled on the den sofa sniffling over a wedding on "The Young and the Restless" when he suddenly remembered Avery Billiot's wedding tomorrow night. The wedding gift – a sterling silver candelabra – sat boxed and wrapped on the dining room table. But Donnie hadn't given a *thought* to his attire for the occasion. He turned off the TV and hurried to his bedroom, throwing open his closets.

In deference to Mrs. Billiot, Donnie Lee decided not to go to the wedding in drag. He did, however, wish to make a fashion statement. So after much rummaging through his finery and discarding several flamboyant outfits, Donnie finally settled on a classic white-on-white tuxedo with white top hat and pearl studs. That little chore taken care of, Donnie dressed himself in orange denim shorts, a white and orange polo shirt, and Mexican leather sandals he'd bought in Taxco. It was such a beautiful day, he decided to get out and wander through the Quarter, maybe meet with a few friends at The Limp Wrist for happy hour. As he was heading out the front door, his parrot, Big Blue, whistled at him. "Pretty boy," he croaked. "Nice tush. Pretty boy."

*****

Avery Billiot was adjusting the flap on top of his lodge when he saw Donnie Lee whiz by in a blur of apple-red BMW and Ralph Lauren cologne. Avery shook his head and chuckled to himself. God made some men "special", he reflected. And Donnie Lee certainly had good company in *this* special neighborhood.

Avery stood back and looked at his work. The lodge was solid; nothing but a hurricane or a tornado would bring it down. He couldn't build a fire in it, though, not inside the city limits. Not that he'd need one this time of year. And he was only sleeping in it for one night – the sleeping bag would do just fine. Late tomorrow night, after the festivities, he and Samantha would be sleeping in the Quarter at the Cornstalk Hotel. Avery would have been happy staying in the lodge for the night, but Samantha said they'd never have a minute of privacy until everybody passed out, and half of his relatives would pass out *in* the lodge. So, in the interest of getting laid on his wedding night, Avery had agreed to the Cornstalk. On Sunday they were leaving for an extended tour of the west, including stops at Chaco Canyon, Mesa Verde and Yosemite. And there were friends and pow wows all along the way; between them they knew at least twenty-five people in every state between Louisiana and California. With all the stops to make and friends to see, Avery speculated they might make it home sometime next year. Samantha asked him if he had anything better to do, and he said not really, which was absolutely the truth.

    Avery had spent sixteen years of his life as an auto mechanic, but for the last ten years he had made a very comfortable living buying land at tax sales. Some he sold, some had homes he renovated and rented out, some land in the northern part of the state had timber leases. He wasn't rich but he no longer had to work for other people, either. The revenues from the land gave him time to make and sell his crafts, tend to Indian business, help his family. He owned a nice little side business with his brother Emile, building pirogues. They were not overworked; they only built about three of the sturdy little boats a year. Emile also owned an upholstery business, which kept him busier than he wanted to be.

Avery was glad to be getting married again. Every time a relationship went sour, he wound up living with his mother again, which wasn't bad – he loved his mother – but he'd felt he had been living in limbo for a long time. He owned six houses he'd never lived in, and property he'd never built on. Marriage to the right woman would surely give him the stability he craved. He knew that simply by accident of birth he came from a long line of displaced persons; Indians had been displaced for several hundred years now. But it was not the *nature* of his people to be displaced; above all else they valued their relationship with Mother Earth. It was time for things to change.

Avery walked into the kitchen in time to hear someone banging on the front door. Uncle Otto was standing on the front porch with a duffel bag and what looked and smelled like a sack of oysters. Uncle Otto was his mother's seventy-nine year old uncle from Golden Meadow. Nothing but weddings and funerals brought him to town. Uncle Otto called New Orleans "Satan's navel". Avery asked him once if New Orleans was Satan's navel, what would he call Baton Rouge? Uncle Otto said, "Satan's crotch. All them politicians think with their balls."

*****

Anthony Guidry stuck his head out of his bedroom door and looked down the hall. The door to the guest room (a/k/a his sister's room) was open. He listened intently but heard nothing. Good. Maybe he was alone in the house. He showered, shaved and dressed, measured his penis for the ten thousandth time, then headed down the long hall to the kitchen at the back of the house. No one was home but it was only a matter of time. He'd better eat fast.

Anthony was bolting down leftover gumbo, crawfish fried rice, turnip greens and Mexican cornbread when he heard the front door slam. "Ant'ny! Ya' home, dahlin'?" His mother's nasal bellow sounded through the house like a tugboat horn. Anthony ignored her and tackled his food with renewed vigor. He heard his mother lumbering down the hallway, panting and wheezing with the effort. She spilled into the kitchen like Godzilla's younger sister, a bag of groceries clutched in each beefy arm.

"There you are, baby. I'm glad to see you eating. You're too skinny, don't got enough meat on your bones. You're lookin' sickly lately, not enough sun. You know, if you stay in your room all the time playin' those video games and listen' to that rock music you'll grow mold in there in the dark. You'd think with you workin' at night you could get out more during the day, go over to the lakefront, get on a softball team."

"Ma, I get out, okay, I go to school, remember?"

Mrs. Guidry ignored her only son as she unloaded her bags – two weeks worth of meat from Glorioso's Meat Market on Magazine Street: pork roast, beef roast, pork chops, two chickens, sausage, ham hocks, ground beef, bacon and three big slabs of cheese. Anthony eyed this butcher's bounty and thought it was no wonder his mother was growing by the day. He reached for the tobasco sauce and tried to concentrate on his food.

"You know ever since your daddy died and went to live with the angels, you don't go fishin' no more, you never take the boat out; you haven't gone hunting in I don't how long. You don't get enough fresh air, Ant'ny. It ain't good for you."

Anthony seriously doubted his father had gone to live with the angels. If there was a poker table with a beer keg on the other side, that's where his father had gone to live. But he had enjoyed his old man's company when he'd been alive, and it was true that Anthony hadn't been able to bring himself to participate in any of the masculine father-and-son pursuits he and Pete Guidry had enjoyed prior to his bizarre death three years ago at the age of fifty-one.

In a cruel twist of fate, Anthony and Pete and Pete's best friend Billy Broussard had gone hunting in the wrong place at the wrong time. They'd gone to Montana on their annual hunting trip, unfortunately during moose rutting season. Pete was five hundred feet or so from the lake, answering nature's call, when a bull moose came out of the lake, took one whiff of Pete, fell in love with him and tried to mount him. Poor, unfortunate Pete. There he was with his pants down and a full grown bull moose trying to perform unnatural acts with him in the middle of a forest in Montana. Pete fought valiantly for his virtue, but he was overwhelmed by the ungainly, fifteen hundred pound creature and expired when the moose sat on him in post-coital bliss. Having thrown down their weapons and run for their lives, Anthony and Billy watched helplessly from the tree they had scaled in absolute terror. After his best friend's misadventure in the woods, Billy had forsaken all outdoor sports and taken up bowling and Cajun dancing. Anthony hadn't been out in the woods since.

"You missed your sister. I gave her money to put down a deposit on a little apartment over on Soniat.. I can't have the two of you under one roof, fighting all the time." Anthony silently thanked all the saints for watching over him. "She saw an ad in the paper, prob'ly one 'a those big houses all cut up. That's such a shame, cuttin' up those beautiful houses the way they do, but they good for people like Tammy. She got a job over by Soledo's Spaghetti House at night, waitressing. She said the money's good. I'm just glad she ain't dancin' nekkid somewhere's in the Quarter." Anthony gagged at the idea of his sister dancing naked. She was a pretty girl but she needed to lose about thirty pounds of baby fat. He couldn't imagine anyone paying a dime to take a peek at Tammy's body, but then she didn't look any worse than some of those girls he'd seen at Fannies or the Full Moon. He wisely kept his thoughts to himself.

Anthony finished his meal as quickly as humanly possible, put his dishes in the dishwasher, then said, "See you later, Ma."

"Where you headed in such a hurry? You ain't got no classes today."

Anthony pulled his keys out of his pocket and trotted to the front door. "Got things to do." Actually he had *nothing* to do, but sitting on a bench in Audubon Park watching the ducks defecate was preferable to staying at home and listening to his mother. He had no classes on Friday, no girlfriend to visit, and his best friend Paul was a mechanic who worked six days a week. He had a couple of other friends from school, Larry and John, but he didn't feel like visiting either of them. Larry's girlfriend was a pain in the ass with big tits and an even bigger mouth. Anthony supposed Larry hung around for the big tits, because it certainly wasn't Charlene's cheerful disposition that kept him at home. John started his day with a joint and a Bud, and while Anthony wasn't averse to a cold brew now and then, he found his friend's increasing alcoholism a bit disturbing. Besides, John's sister Candi lived with him, and every time he went over there, she was wandering around half naked, changing her shirt in front of him, bending over and showing her big ole butt, shit like that. He wouldn't normally mind gazing upon half-naked women, but she looked like a younger version of his mother and he just couldn't face it this morning. Anthony made a quick mental review of his friends and decided it was time for his social life to move in a different direction.

Anthony was in a rut and depressed. His work/school schedules permitted little free time and were murder on his love life, not to mention the drawbacks of living with his mother. He was in his second year at Delgado in the auto mechanics program and would graduate soon, but he couldn't look for a mechanic's job until he graduated, so he was stuck working nights at the grocery store. All of which severely limited his opportunities to meet girls, since few women ever took the auto mechanics program, and the only girls he saw at the grocery store were either in a hurry or married or not up to his aesthetic standards. And if he did meet someone, he couldn't exactly bring them home to get romantic in his mother's house. He decided to drive around and look at "for rent" signs.

Anthony had saved a good bit of money the last year, since some of the money from his father's life insurance policy was paying for his education and his mother refused to let him pay for anything at home. He actually made good money at the grocery store, and he still had quite a bit left out of his share of his dad's life insurance policy. He could afford his own apartment and it was time to rent one. Today. He needed to stop mourning the loss of Debbie and get on with his life.

Until a year ago, Anthony had lived for eleven months with Debbie Breaux, a Hooters waitress, in a double on Coliseum Street. He had met her while working out at the YMCA and had fallen in lust with her luscious body encased in pink leotards; four weeks later they were living together. Things hadn't been perfect – their schedules didn't allow them to spend much time together – but Anthony was happy with the little time they had. Apparently, Debbie wasn't, and one night while Anthony was at work, Debbie ran off to New Iberia with some guy named Jimmy who worked offshore on an oil rig, leaving Anthony with a note, four pieces of furniture, and a three hundred dollar phone bill. He heard through the grapevine that Debbie and Jimmy had gotten married at Christmas and were divorced by Valentine's Day. Anthony was heartbroken when she left, but found solace in the fact that her marriage had lasted only six weeks. She had tried to call Anthony last month, but his mother had answered the phone and told Debbie that Anthony was through with her devil worshipping little ass and not to call her house again. Anthony was actually relieved to have missed her call; he did not want to go back to her in a weak moment. It was time to move on to new territory.

Anthony drove around through the neighborhoods, mentally rejecting all the rentals where he saw signs. He wasn't being overly picky, having considered just one big room, but realistically he needed a small double with a driveway; he was tired of working on his car in the street. After an hour of slowly cruising the narrow streets, he was about to give up and get a newspaper when he saw it, the perfect place, a little blue shotgun double with driveways on both sides and sheds in the back. Anthony pulled up in front, got out of the car and looked at the sign. "For rent, 1 B/R, 1 ba., LR,

DR, driveway, shed, sm. back yd., water pd, $550/mo. Knock next door." He stood on the porch and knocked at the door on the left. A beautiful redheaded apparition in paint-splotched overall shorts and a tube top came to the door holding a paintbrush. She smiled brightly. "You here about the apartment next door?" Anthony nodded, suddenly tongue-tied. "I'm Amy; I own the house. Excuse my appearance, I was just painting the kitchen. Come on in." As he crossed Amy's threshold, Anthony decided then and there that he had found his new home.

*****

Dave Richard stood in front of the big green house a block off St. Charles, hoping to God and all the saints that the interior of Dr. Mayeaux' house did not resemble Boxcar's house from hell. He crossed himself, then ascended the front steps and rang the doorbell. After a few minutes a thickset woman in a maid's uniform answered the door. Dave gave her his card and said he was there to inspect and photograph the house and put up the for sale sign. She let him in but shook her head. "Doctor no tell me about no pictures or nothin'," she said, "but I don't care much, I quitting anyway, I jus' need to get paid. That cheap sona'bitch no pay me yet. I ain't workin' in this nuthouse no more. I seen plenty in Honduras, but I never seen nothin' before like what goes on this house, no sir, gettin' my ass outta here!"

Dave stood in bewildered silence for a moment, then said, "Come again?"

"I just get here to this city, I only work for him two weeks; I hear funny things, I see funny things, but I mind my own business, you understan'."

Dave nodded, but he didn't understand a goddamn thing she just said. "Uh, maybe this is a bad time," he mumbled and turned to leave.

The maid grabbed his arm and said, "No, doan go, I think I need help with something. I wanna show you something I find this mornin' when I get here. I ain't so sure what to do. I am just the maid here, and I no be in this country long, so maybe you can tell me what to do about this here. You come with me, I show you."

Totally perplexed, Dave followed the maid through the front parlor and up the stairs, where she led him to a door in the back of the house on the second floor. The door was padlocked, but he could hear a thumping sound on the other side of the wall, like someone beating on the floor. "Is anybody in there?" he called out. More thumping and something that sounded like clanking. Dave reflected that if he were Steven Segal he would kick the door in. Clint Eastwood would probably shoot the lock off. But Dave was no foolhardy hero, he did what any sane American would do in this situation, he pulled his cell phone out of his pocket and called the police. While he and the maid, whose name was Consuela, stood in the hall, listening to more

Just Off the Streetcar Line

thumping, waiting for the police to show up, he asked her what she thought was in there.

"I doan know, but it might be a beeg animal, somethin' like that."

Dave scratched his head. "A dog maybe?"

"I doan hear no barkin', jus' bangin'." About that time something banged against the wall again.

"Well there sure is something alive in there!" said Dave.

The maid started down the stairs. "Le's go wait for the police. I is a'scared a' whatever be in there."

Dave and Consuela had just sat down on the front steps when two police cars pulled up in front of the house. A tall, burley black man who bore an eerie resemblance to O.J. Simpson got out of one car with a tall, thin white woman whom Dave presumed to be his partner. Two middle-aged white men stepped out of the other car. "You the guy who called about a disturbance?" asked O.J.

"I'm the guy," Dave answered. "But it isn't exactly a disturbance; we don't know *what* it is. Come on in, see for yourself." They all trooped up to the second floor and looked at the padlocked door. The thumping and clanking sounds continued unabated.

"What's in there?" the female officer asked.

"Don't know," said Dave, "but it's alive, whatever it is."

O.J. drew his gun and told Dave and Consuela to stand clear of the door. They hid in the alcove down the hall. O.J. shot off the lock and slowly opened the door. "Holy shit!" he said softly. They all crowded behind O.J. to have a look. "Jesus God!" said one of the middle-aged officers. Dave had nothing to say — his mouth was hanging to his knees. Behind the wooden door was a wrought-iron gate; through the bars they could see a young blonde woman, her mouth taped shut and her wrists chained to an iron bedframe. She had a bruise on her left cheek, she was naked, and she was quite agitated. O.J. shot off the lock on the iron gate and they all tumbled inside the room. The female cop pulled the tape off the poor woman's mouth, O.J. shot off the locks on the chain, and one of the other cops covered the blonde woman with a sheet. The blonde started screaming bloody murder about "killing that fucking bastard" and cutting his balls off with a rusty knife, which she also threatened to stick up his ass. There were more very vocal and descriptive threats, but most were of the same ilk. The audience definitely got the impression that this poor woman very badly wanted Dr. Mayeaux dismembered while still alive, preferably in public.

"Ma'am, did Dr. Arnold Mayeaux lock you in here and leave you like this?" asked O.J. while his female partner called for an ambulance.

Just Off the Streetcar Line

"You're goddamn right he did, that filthy fucking son of a warthog!" More loud invectives followed concerning the ancestry of Dr. Mayeaux. Then the blonde, who said her name was Linda, started to cry. She alternately cried and cursed and at one point threw the bedside lamp against the wall. Dave kept muttering "holy Jesus" and stared at the poor woman, who said she'd been locked up in there since last night.

O.J. told the maid to find something alcoholic, something *strong*, and be quick about it. Consuela ran out and returned a few minutes later with a bottle of Crown Royal. Linda Lewis took a big swig from the bottle, coughed and sputtered, then took another swig. In the meantime, one of the middle-aged cops called the station to request a photographer and somebody named Lester. A request was also put in to pick up Dr. Mayeaux at his clinic near Touro Infirmary, which brought on another spate of screaming and cursing from Linda.

The ambulance arrived, but they couldn't take Linda to Charity Hospital until the photographer showed up, so they treated her wounds, which were minor, and O.J. questioned her once the brandy started to take effect and she had calmed down a little. She said Dr. Mayeaux had picked her up at a bar on Magazine Street, gotten her drunk, then brought her to his house. He then took her up to this room, punched her in the face when she refused to enter, and dragged her by the hair into the room. She fought back but he overpowered her and handcuffed her face-down to the bed frame. When she kicked him in the face, he tied her feet to the footboard. He then beat her with a leather strap and sodomized her. He raped her a couple more times during the night, and when he left sometime in the morning, he untied her feet but left her chained to the bed with her mouth taped.

Dave sat in a chair and listened to her tale in stunned silence. He had never heard of such a thing; he thought this stuff only happened in the movies! At some point he realized he'd lost the sale of the house, but it was almost a comic afterthought.

While they were all waiting for the photographer and the mysterious Lester, Dave had a few minutes to look around the room. He hadn't seen anything like this even in porno movies. There were handcuffs, paddles, belts, a fly swatter, a spiked collar, a leash, and a riding crop hanging from hooks in the wall; there was a rope dangling from the ceiling, a policeman's uniform thrown over a chair. Dave noticed that in one corner a Howdy Doody doll sat astride a saddle placed on top of a wooden sawhorse, and in another corner was a mannequin decked out like the Lone Ranger. A nurse's uniform and nun's habit were placed on hangars and hung from a steel bar suspended from the ceiling. There was also a table covered with dildos (assorted colors and sizes), strings of Mardi Gras beads, boxes of condoms, and several little rubber toys, including a mouse, a snake, a giraffe and a dolphin. He was a bit perplexed by the Richard Nixon mask and the Barbie doll, but completely understood the usefulness of the little plastic bats, the kind thrown from Mardi Gras floats. There were a few objects on the table that totally mystified Dave, but he didn't want to ask anybody what they were. He didn't want to appear unsophisticated.

The cop named Lester finally arrived with a photographer and a man who dusted for fingerprints and gathered other evidence. Lester wandered around with his hands in his pockets, examining the contents of the room, muttering "one sick puppy we got here." The photographer chewed gum and took pictures. He looked at Dave and said, "Takes all kinds, huh bro'?" Dave just nodded silently. Lester took Dave's statement and told him he could go but asked for a business card, which Dave immediately supplied then left the house, very relieved to finally get the hell out of there. He went straight home, poured himself a shot of bourbon and tossed it back. After six more shots he laid down on the couch in the den for a short nap. Judy found him still there six hours later, snoring like a banshee, so she just left him where he lay. He awoke at midnight, somewhat disoriented. He stumbled upstairs, tumbled into bed in his clothes, and patted Judy on the ass. "Good night, dear," he mumbled.

Judy stirred sleepily. "Tough day?" she asked.

"You have no idea," Dave answered, then fell back asleep immediately.

*****

Graham Fellows sat outside of PJ's coffeehouse on the Tulane campus, nursing a mild hangover and sipping a tall, frothy cafe-au-lait. He was more tired than hung over, and he knew he needed lunch more than coffee, but right now the coffee tasted better than a steak.

Graham and Isabella had made love into the wee hours, finally falling asleep around four o'clock. He just barely made his eleven o'clock class, which he cut short. He had one more class at three, then he was finished for the day. He had not called Marsha and had no plans to do so. He also had no plans to go back to the house he rarely shared with her until tomorrow when he played out his little charade with Victor. There was nothing there that he needed, and he was not going to go back to that house and try to deal with his loony tunes wife on any sort of rational level. She could sit there and go into fits of apoplexy for all he cared. He just wanted to go back to his condo in the Quarter, have a quiet dinner somewhere with Isabella, maybe see a movie, have drinks. He would think about it later. Right now he just wanted to do a little girl watching and kill some time.

The campus coffeehouse is an excellent place for girl watching. To be sure, there is a sizable contingency of the hairy-legged and fluffy armpit crowd, but the bulk of Tulane's female population is young, pretty and feminine, and due to New Orleans' consistently warm, muggy climate, they prefer to stroll around with two-thirds of their lovely young, often

Just Off the Streetcar Line

pierced and tattooed, carcasses exposed most of the year. This is no uptight northeast knee sock and blazer campus – more like *Charmed* meets *Animal House*.

Sitting at his little table drinking coffee and occasionally glancing at the *Times-Picayune*, Graham was desperately trying to appear nonchalant, but he almost dumped his coffee in has lap when two young girls dropped their books on the table next to him and sat down. At first glance, he thought the little blonde was wearing a pair of green bib overalls with absolutely nothing underneath. Upon closer inspection, however, he noticed that she had two large frog decals pasted over her nipples. Her friend, who sported short, spiky dyed black hair, black fingernail polish, and black and silver combat boots, was wearing a pair of ultra-short shorts that showed a large tongue tattooed on her left hip; her skimpy little spaghetti-strapped tee-shirt that exposed her navel ring also exposed most of her D-cup breasts and the little ladybug tattoo hovering just above her right nipple. Graham, who by now had a hard-on the size of an eggplant, couldn't help but overhear their conversation.

"So did you notice my new tattoo?" asked Ms. Combat Boots, pointing at her ladybug.

"Too cute! Is it, like, sitting on your nipple?"

She shook her spiky head. "Uh-uh. I had him put a little bee right under the nipple, see?" She pulled down the right side of her shirt to show off the little bee and a pretty pink nipple. Graham's hand shook and he spilled coffee on his paper. He looked around him and could not believe that he was the only person watching this little peep show. Everyone else was engrossed in their books and papers.

"Way cute, girlfriend! How do you like my froggies?"

"Very cool." Ms. Boots leaned across the table and unhooked one of the bib straps, totally exposing one of the frogs to the bright sunshine. "Ribbit," she said, casually pinching the frog's midsection. Graham saw the frog's stomach swell and felt his penis go into overdrive.

Ms. Froggie glanced down at her breast and giggled. "Radical! It's, like, porno hillbillie."

Ms. Boots giggled. "You've missed your calling, Babe." She leaned back and stretched, her nipples straining against her tee-shirt. "So what'd'ya wanna do tonight?"

"I thought we could, like, go down to Quarter and, like, try out our new fake ID's, like, try to get into The Dungeon."

"Aw, nobody I know goes to the Dungeon anymore. Let's get Bridget and Sandy and go down to Bourbon Street. Let them buy the drinks – they're legal. We could go stand outside Puddin' Pie and watch the gay guys moon the tourists, then go over to La

Just Off the Streetcar Line

Bamba's and dance. That place is always fulla hot bods."

"Cool." Ms. Froggie was casually jiggling her exposed breast. "Do you think my boobs are, like, too small? Like, maybe I need implants." Graham choked on his coffee.

Ms. Boots shook her spiky head and casually squeezed Miss Froggie's left breast. "No way. You have very perky boobs. Tinkerbell boobs." The analogy was lost on Graham, who was nonetheless very appreciative of Ms. Froggie's perky little boobs. "Besides, you don't wanna fuck up your boobs. Remember that girl from psych class? Becky. Hers came out lopsided, man. I mean, like, they pointed in different directions for weeks. She had to have them redone."

Ms. Froggie sighed and looked down at her rather normal breasts and said wistfully, "I guess you're right. But, like, I just wish I had boobs like yours. Like, maybe I'd get noticed more."

Ms. Boots grinned and tweaked her friend's frog again. "Believe me, you'll get noticed in this outfit." Graham fervently agreed. "Besides, you're cute. Guys like cute. Now look at me, I'm not cute."

"But you're beautiful! You look just like Angelina Jolie."

"Thanks, sweetie, but guys don't look at my face, they look at my tits. I am so sick of guys talking to my fucking tits!"

Ms. Froggie sighed again. "I wish I had that problem." She looked at her Kermit-the-Frog wristwatch. "You know what, like, tonight's a long way off. I'm bored. Let's, like, do something now."

"Reggie and Brian are still at my apartment. They're recovering from last night's fuckathon. We could go over and play strip poker." She grinned and licked her black lips. "First one to lose their clothes gets a group tongue lashing."

"Do my frogs count as clothing?"

"Only if you let me pull them off with my teeth."

Ms. Froggie giggled again. "Cool." They gathered their books and headed off down Freret Street. Graham casually laid his newspaper across his lap and waited for the swelling to go down.

*****

Miss Beulah was adding the finishing touches to her voodoo doll. It was a special doll for Avery and his bride, designed to keep the bride and groom together in married bliss for the rest of their lives, or at least for as long as the doll stayed in their home. If the doll is ever removed from the house, look out! There's trouble brewing, especially if the doll is removed by a wanton woman.

It was a beautiful doll, adorned with orange silk, pink feathers and yellow beads, with an elaborate green headdress and a little purple umbrella in the doll's left hand. Miss Beulah arose from her armchair with a grunt and carried the doll over to her alter in the hallway, where she performed a purification ritual, passing the doll through cedar and sage smoke and sprinkling it with rosewater. She then christened it Belinda and stuck its feet in a little chunk of green clay. "Keeps the feet from wanderin' down into darkness," she mumbled. Then she carefully wrapped the doll in white tissue paper and placed it in a blue oblong box which she topped with a silver bow. That little chore taken care of, Miss Beulah hobbled out to the kitchen to check on the big pot of gumbo she'd left simmering on the stove.

The giant cauldron was slowly bubbling next to a big pot of collard greens and ham hocks. On the back burners sat a slightly smaller pot of butterbeans and a pot of green beans with peppers and sausage. Miss Beulah opened the oven door and examined the four loaves of pumpkin bread. "They's comin' along, comin' along jest fine." She then turned her attention to the catfish slowly frying in the electric skillet. "Oh yes, nice an' brown, nice an' brown. Ya'll can come outta there now." While the fish were draining on paper towels, she cut up tomatoes and set them next to the deviled eggs in the refrigerator. She turned off all her pots, checked the rice cooker, then pulled the loaves out of the oven. "Yes indeed, we gonna eat good tonight. Nobody in my house gonna go hongry." Nobody in Miss Beulah's house would ever go hungry. As it was, they were all at least thirty pounds overweight, except for her granddaughter, who was a skinny little thing.

Clarice came running in from the back yard, all excited and breathless. "Grandmamma, Miss Prissy has new kittens in the shed!"

Miss Beulah ladled gumbo into a plastic container and wrapped up half a pumpkin bread loaf in a plastic bag. "Miss Prissy done been blessed again." She placed the food in a paper bag. "Here baby girl, take this bag over to li'l Jackie. Poor little thang's mama goes off and leaves her home by herself and she don't eat nothin' but pizzas. I know 'cause I seen that pizza delivery car over there most ever' night for a week. You take this over there, and be careful wif' it. Don't drop it and spill nothin'."

"Yes, ma'am, I'll be careful." She scooted out the back door with her bag of goodies.

Miss Beulah ambled into the dining room to set the table, muttering to herself. "Dat Lisa don't got the sense God give a billy goat. And that little Jackie don't got nobody else neither. She always tryin' to take ker 'o her mama and that ain't right, no suh, her mama oughta be taking' ker o' her baby. She ain't had no sense her whole entire life. Musta been dropped on her head when she was borned." She looked up at the clock on the sideboard. Almost time for her daughter and husband to come home from work. Her son was out looking for a job, but he would be home soon, too; he knew better than to miss dinner.

Elijah would be coming home from work for the last time this evening. After thirty-two years with the Sewerage and Water Board, he was retiring today. His retirement party was being held next Tuesday night at Pampy's restaurant on Broad Street.

Yolanda was a secretary in a big law firm downtown. Much to the delight of her parents, Yolanda and Clarice had moved in with Beulah and Elijah after Yolanda's husband Harry had left her for an exotic dancer. Poor Harry. After six months with the dancer, he had come down with a mysterious illness that left him impotent. After the dancer left him for a more virile young man, Harry had shown up at Miss Beulah's door, accusing her of "puttin' the hoodoo" on him. Miss Beulah told him he got what he deserved and chased him away with a broom. Yolanda just stood on the porch and laughed at him and told him she hoped his dingaling fell off.

Leroy was out looking for work. Miss Beulah was confident that he would find a good job, not only because Leroy was an experienced forklift driver but because Miss Beulah had wrapped a dollar bill in a chicken bone this afternoon, burned it in a kettle and planted the ashes under an oak tree with a liberty silver dollar. Leroy needed all the help he could get. Miss Beulah had already told her wayward but penitent son that if he ever drank another drop of alcohol that she would turn him into a toad, and he absolutely believed her. He would never drink another drop.

Elijah opened the front door and dropped his cap on the hat tree in the front room. "Well, woman, I am home for good."

Miss Beulah walked over to him and kissed his cheek. "Thank the lawd."

*****

Eugenia Robichaux was going through her cavernous pantry, placing jars in a box. Tigger lay on his back against the door. "Yeah, Tigger, that's gonna be some humdinger of a wedding, boy. Ever'body takin' something to eat. Me, I'm gonna take a big basket of fried soft shell crabs. There ain't nobody don't like them crabs; got to be some kinda heathen not to like them crabs. Avery's mama gonna be lookin' for a place to hide, come tomorrow night. I told her, anybody needs a place to sleep, send 'em over, I got plenty room. She said she's only sendin' over the sober ones. Her cousin Nadia gonna stay over here, and Nadia's daughter Euphrasia. You remember Euphrasia, Tigger; she's the one got big ole feet like pirogues. She could paddle her way across the bayou with them feet o' hers." Tigger scratched his ear and shook his head violently, then sneezed.

Eugenia pulled more mason jars from shelves. "I'm gonna give Avery and Samantha this box a' stuff I put up, a jar each of ever'thing I got here. Let's see, we got tomatoes, corn relish, bread 'n butter pickles, fig preserves, pickled peaches, blackberry jam, banana peppers, okra, red pepper jelly, blueberries, boysenberry jelly, apple butter, watermelon pickles, strawberries with green peppers, and some peach and onion salsa. That's all this box is gonna hold, Tigger."

She dragged the box through the hallway and into the living room, then stood and looked down at it. "You know, I should'a wrapped this box before I filled it." She pulled out all the jars and set them on the floor, then went looking for wrapping paper. She pulled out rolls of paper and a big bag of ribbons and bows. "Can't use this stuff, Tigger, it's got little kittens all over it. Must'a been left over from Marsha Billiot's baby shower." She pulled out a roll of paper covered with wild animals. "Can't use this stuff, neither. That was for Yolanda's birthday party last fall. You remember, I gave her that pretty red sweater set. Now I could use this pink paper with the hearts. What'a you think, Tigger?" Tigger flopped down on the floor and sighed. "No, I guess you right. This ain't no Valentine's Day." She rummaged around some more and finally came up with a roll of gold foil paper with green pinstripes and some purple bows. "Them's some purty Mardi Gras colors, Tigger. That'll work." Eugenia and Tigger wandered back into the living room. While she wrapped the box and box top, Eugenia prattled on about her visit to Lakeside Mall. Tigger lay on his back with his paws in the air and his tongue lolling out.

"I'm tellin' you, Tigger, that mall is somethin' else again. They got more stuff than you an' me ever wanna buy and it all cost *some money*, son. They got plenty stores in there, but I couldn't find *nothin'*. I looked at sheets and towels and kitchen stuff, but I don't know what Avery and Samantha's got between 'em. I looked at some a' that useless silver stuff. I'll tell you, Tigger, I ain't payin' no two hunnert dollars for some tray that you got to polish all the time anyway. And I ask you, who needs a silver bread basket?" Tigger sneezed rapidly three times and stood up. "Exactly. A plain old palmetto basket's good enough. You just tryin' to keep the biscuits warm anyway. Well, I look and I look. Nothin'. I got so tired a' lookin' I just sat down on a bench and watched the people go by."

Eugenia looked over at Tigger, who was sitting up scratching fleas in his ear. "Let me tell you, boy, they got some strange people out there in that mall, not like regular people who live around here. Man, I saw girls with purple hair and earrings in their noses and above their eyebrows and one girl with about six holes in her ear. If it rains I guess her ears is gonna leak. And the tattoos! Man, you should'a seen them tattoos. *Girls* with tattoos, Tigger, not no sailors, no siree. I counted eight tattoos on one little girl. She had green hair, too, all stickin' up on her head, looked just like one a' them troll dolls. She was talkin' to another little girl about tattooin' her butt. I'd like to tattoo her butt; I'd write "fool" all the way across her behind. And them girls don't wear hardly no clothes, neither. Their skirts is so short you can see what color their drawers are. And little bitty shirts that don't cover their belly buttons and their little boobies hangin' out all over the place. And talk about belly buttons, Tigger, some a' them young ladies got earrings stuck in their belly buttons! Man, I never seen nothin' like it."

Eugenia finished her wrapping and started placing the jars back in the box. "Well, Tigger, it'd been a long time since I'd been in that mall, and they'll be throwin' dirt over me before I go back. I saw some sights in there I don't plan to see again. There were some young boys in there – *boys*, Tigger – wearing black fingernail polish and black lipstick! Wearin' all black like they was some kinda' vampires. And those girls with their little short skirts wearing big ole combat boots like they was soldiers. Just looked ridiculous to me, but I don't know nothin' about fashion. Ain't never seen nothin' like it in my life. I told Nadine, you got to get me outta this place before I get attacked! Looked like some kinda people zoo."

Eugenia absently scratched Tigger under his chin. "You shoulda seen the big ole girls in there, Tigger. I never seen so many people who need to go on a diet. I know I need to lose me about twenty pounds myself, but man, we talkin' about women who weighs three hunnert pounds! I don't know how they walk, Tigger. They look like big ole elephants. It's sad, woman let herself go like that. Lotta young girls, too. Well, I decided I didn't want nothin' in that mall and come home and looked in my pantry." Eugenia left the box in the middle of the floor. "Michel can pick that up when he come back from the bayou tomorrow, it's too heavy for the likes of me. Let's go fix dinner, Tigger. We havin' fried chicken tonight." Tigger followed her into the kitchen, where he took up sentry under the table.

*****

Louie's investigation of Danny Darrow took less than an hour. He called Lenny Leaper, his best friend since high school. Lenny was a hacker, a computer whiz who'd been fired from several jobs and arrested more than once, but the charges never stuck – the evidence always mysteriously disappeared after Lenny made bail each time. Lenny finally opened a security business, which had been flourishing for the last four years, and a couple of side businesses, including an on-line dating service and e-LIPS, a soft-porn web site. Lenny could hack into any computer system on earth (and probably had); he was Louie's most valuable resource.

Through Lenny, Louie found out that Danny Darrow's real name was Gerry O'Hara (a/k/a Gerald Flannery, a/k/a Matthew Connery, a/k/a Michael Cross); born November 3, 1959 in Chicago to Irish nationals Richard and Caitlin O'Hara (importers); carried dual citizenship; lived from age four to age ten in Derry (a/k/a Londonderry), then back to Chicago until age fifteen; attended high school in Derry for a year, then back to Chicago for four years; received a degree in business from Northwestern. He had worked since college for Gilhooley, Ltd., an import/export business owned by his uncle Michael Gilhooley, headquartered in Derry, with offices in London, Amsterdam, Chicago and Nassau, Grand Bahamas. Since joining Gilhooley, Ltd., the erstwhile Mr. Darrow-O'Hara-Flannery-Connery-Cross had become quite a globetrotter, visiting not only London, Amsterdam, and Nassau, but also Mexico, Peru, Argentina, Cuba, Libya, the Cayman Islands, Jordan, Italy, Algeria and the Czech Republic. Interpol was extremely interested in the activities of the O'Hara's and the Gilhooley's, who were suspected smugglers, gunrunners and IRA terrorists.

Louie sat and looked at the fax sheets set out before him, which included photographs and several (he was certain) purloined documents. All he could say was "my, my, my." He wasn't sure exactly what to tell Millie, however; just because a man is a terrorist doesn't necessarily mean he's a golddigger. After all, he seemed to do quite well for himself and his family was not exactly poverty-stricken. The poor schmuck might actually be in love with Veronica, and Louie hated to interfere with true love. But then, his client had paid him to dig up whatever he could about Veronica's boyfriend, so he felt obligated to show her what he had. After that, it was up to Veronica whether or not to continue dating a terrorist.

The only thing that really nagged Louie was why Mr. IRA would tell so many obviously unnecessary lies (i.e., the New York connection) rather than just saying he's from Chicago, a city he knew well. It's just too hard to keep lying about something unfamiliar; you eventually get caught. Either the guy was trying to distance himself from Chicago, or he just wasn't very bright. Or maybe he was a compulsive liar. Maybe all three, which made him a dumb, unreliable IRA terrorist with an identity problem. But that still didn't mean he wasn't in love with Veronica.

Character analysis aside, Louie wondered what the hell Mr. IRA was doing in Louisiana. He sighed and shook his head. Shit rolled downhill, and given enough momentum, a lot of it eventually wound up in New Orleans. His home town was an international port city and a jumping off point for all sorts of nuts and weirdoes with a mission, like those guys back in the eighties who tried to take over some island country. They were caught at the Port of New Orleans with a boatload of guns; turned out they were white supremacists from Alabama. Louie never did understand why they didn't try to leave from Mobile, but of course, New Orleans is more glamorous. As a New Orleanian, Louie would never understand a desire to live in Alabama or even visit what he called the "ding-dong state". His experience with Alabama was confined mainly to barreling through it, preferably in the dark, at 85 m.p.h. on his way to Florida.

Louie had visited Bellingrath Gardens once, though, ten years ago with his cousin Coceaux, his father's older sister's daughter, when her yacht was anchored in Mobile Bay for a few days for minor repairs and she had time to kill. Coceaux had invited Louie to sail with her to Bermuda, but he was in the middle of a hot case, so instead of indulging in a leisurely trip to Bermuda, he'd gone to Mobile and taken a small boat out to the yacht, where he'd found Coceaux sunbathing in an emerald green sequined bikini, drinking Bloody Mary's and eating oysters.

The yacht belonged to Coceaux's husband of (then) twenty years, Jacques Montagne, a rich Frenchman who had been traveling in the Far East at the time. Jacques had made an enormous amount of money manufacturing sex toys and had since branched out into the porno movie business, increasing his annual revenues by three hundred and fifty percent. Coceaux, who was then only forty-five and still a raving beauty (and at fifty-five now looked like an older Catherine Zeta-Jones), consoled herself with screwing most of her crew. At her request, Louie took her to Bellingrath Gardens, which she thought were beautiful but boring. She said she was tired of sitting on the yacht watching idiot rednecks get drunk and try to operate speedboats, so he offered to take her to the Grand Hotel at Point Clear, which she nixed as too stuffy, so he took her to Dauphin Island, where they were lucky enough to get a room in a little motel across the street from the beach. They sat on the sand in the dark and ate fried chicken out of a bucket and drank numerous bottles of German beer. They talked about Paris, where Coceaux lived in relative splendor with Jacques, and Rome, where she lived off and on with Rudolfo, her long-time lover, who sometimes lived in Florence with his wife, who spent most of *her* time in Naples with *her* lover, a well-known Greek opera singer who had a wife and six children in Athens. Jacques spent most of his time traveling, sometimes with Coceaux, of whom he was genuinely fond, but more often with very young, leggy women he fell madly in love with for a few weeks or months at a time.

After disposing of the chicken bucket and the beer bottles, Louie and Coceaux walked on the beach and groped each other in the dark, then returned to their motel room, where they had sex on every available surface of the room, including up against the walls. Louie adored Coceaux. She was the reason his relationships with other women never worked out, the reason none had ever lasted for more than about a seven or eight month stretch. He might fall in lust, but he would never fall in love with anyone else. Louie's heart belonged to Coceaux.

Louie and Coceaux had been lovers since he was twenty-one and she was thirty-one. For his twenty-first birthday, Louie's mother had given him ten thousand dollars for the vacation destination of his choice, so he decided to visit the Cote d'Azure, where Coceaux was spending the summer in a rented villa in Nice, while Jacques toiled at his factory in Hong Kong, living high in the hills with the eighteen-year-old toy du jour. When Louie called Coceaux to discuss his travel plans, she invited him to spend the summer with her. His mother thought that was a splendid idea, and so did he, since he and Coceaux had always been fairly close and he thought she was beyond cool. Besides, staying in her villa would save him a bundle and he could keep most of his birthday money.

Louie let Coceaux seduce him the second night of his visit (he put up absolutely no resistance), and for the rest of the summer they screwed their way up and down the Cote d'Azure, Coceaux being a restless spirit who would never be content to let the grass grow under her feet for more than a week. They had spent the last twenty-four summers together (and any other times they could arrange). Louie loved her dearly, but their lifestyles and long-range goals were poles apart. So Coceaux continued to circle the globe and Louie continued to work in New Orleans and save for his retirement, which he intended to start the day after his fiftieth birthday (he considered fifty the beginning of his twilight years). Louie wanted to retire to Key West and do as little as possible; Coceaux wanted to continue her love affair with plastic surgery and globe-trotting until she dropped. But even though their goals were miles apart, they truly loved each other, they were the best of friends, and they often discussed spending their golden years together. The fact that they were first cousins never occurred to them as an obstacle – they weren't going to have children together and their families never interfered in their lives at all. In fact, their families were so oblivious to everything but their own dysfunctional lives that no one but Louie's mother even knew about their affair. And that had happened completely by accident, a result of one of her own dysfunctional affairs.

Louie's mother had run into Louie and Coceaux one July morning eight years ago as they were strolling arm-in-arm in Cannes, looking in shop windows, when they stopped to share a kiss under an awning. Louie looked up to see his mother staring at him from ten feet away, obviously surprised. Her only reaction, however, was to say that she had no idea that Louie was in France, but since he was, how about having lunch with her and her friend Vassily? During lunch, it became obvious that Vivienne and Vasilly were traveling through Europe together, but Louie, who had no more than a passing interest in his mother's personal life, ignored their relationship, just as his mother ignored the obvious romance between her son and her niece. The two geriatric lovebirds wound up spending the night with Louie and Coceaux on Coceaux' yacht, then left the next day for Venice.

Neither Louie nor Coceaux would ever want for money. When his parents died, Louie would inherit everything, but money had never meant a great deal to Louie, who could happily live in a shack on the beach. Coceaux would inherit everything when Jacques died, and he would almost certainly predecease her, since he was over twenty years her senior. No matter what type of lifestyles they chose, money would never be a serious issue. And since Rudolpho had died two years ago, Louie and Coceaux had grown even closer. Spending their "twilight" years together was starting to look like a reality for both of them. In fact, as soon as he'd wrapped up the current case, Louie was closing his house/office for the summer and heading off to the

Costa del Sol, where he was meeting Coceaux. From there they would sail to Ibizia, Monte Carlo, the Greek Isles, and Istanbul. Jacques was currently cooling his heels in Rio with last year's Miss Venezuela.

With thoughts of the Mediterranean swimming in his head, Louie called Millie and left a message that he wanted to meet with her, then stuck the folder back in his filing cabinet and locked the drawer. He wanted to wrap up this case and get on with his love life.

*****

Lucille and Leola emptied their bags onto Leola's front room sofa and examined the contents: one bow, one leather quiver with three arrows, one twelve-inch dreamcatcher, one ten-inch drum decorated with painted Kokopelli's, one pueblo-type incense burner with assorted incense packets, one Carlos Nakai CD, two matching pairs of silver and turquoise turtle stud earrings for the bride and groom (both had pierced ears), a book entitled *Tecumsah* and one large poster of Geronimo. The Native American store in the Quarter had been having a going-out-of-busines sale and they had cleaned up.

"Lucille, I do not understand why you just had to buy that bow and arrow set. Avery is not going on the warpath any time soon."

"He might go hunting with it, you never know. Besides, it was such a deal I couldn't pass it up."

Leola sniffed. "You couldn't bring down a rabbit with those arrows, much less a deer. They look mighty flimsy to me."

"Well it isn't like he's going buffalo hunting. The only buffalo around here are in the zoo. He can hang it on his wall."

Leola look doubtful. "Well, I just hope they don't open their presents tomorrow night. If some of those drunken relatives of his get ahold of these arrows, somebody's gonna get hurt."

Lucille giggled. "Let's give 'em to Livonia for crowd control."

"She's going to need something. Remember Mardi Gras day? About thirty people showed up, most of 'em loaded to their eyebrows. That Ricky Dardard even built a fire in the backyard trying to cook hotdogs on a stick and melted one of Livonia's plastic flamingoes. It's a wonder he didn't burn down all that bamboo in the corner of the yard. And those cousins of hers from Violet brought over their Catahoula and got him drunk on Dixie beer. I've never seen a dog drink beer like that before. He just lapped it up. Bet they've been givin' him beer for years, poor thing."

Lucille held the dreamcatcher up to the light. "It was a sight. That dog threw up and defecated all over every yard in the neighborhood. And then that Randy, the little skinny one from Grand Bois, hung himself on a tree limb going after a squirrel. Avery had to climb up there and cut the beads off his neck to get him down. He looked just like a little monkey hanging up there in the rain tree. Lucky he didn't choke to death."

"He looks like a monkey anyway, poor baby, and he's not too bright. I swear, Livonia has some of the ugliest relatives."

Lucille was sniffing the incense package. "Oh, they're not any uglier than anybody else's relatives. Look at your cousin Marshall. He looks just like Buster Keaton."

"Wasn't he an Indian?"

"Marshall? I don't know, he's your cousin."

"Not Marshall, Buster Keaton."

Lucille was inserting an arrow into the bowstring and taking a bead on the mailman through the open window. "I thought Buster Keaton was Jewish."

Leola grabbed the arrow and put it back in the quiver. "I swear somebody's gonna get shot with an arrow before the weekend's over. Well, I heard he was Indian."

Lucille unfurled the poster of Geronimo. "Avery? He *is* Indian, he's Choctaw."

"Not Avery, Buster Keaton. And he's a Houma, not a Choctaw."

Lucille looked blankly at her best friend. "Buster Keaton wasn't Houma, he was Jewish."

"*Avery's* a Houma, not Buster Keaton. Keep up, Lucille." Leola picked up the Carlos Nikai CD and examined the cover. "He sure is a good looking man."

"Buster Keaton?! He was homely as a cowpie."

"Not Buster Keaton, Carlos Nakai."

Lucille examined the CD cover. "He doesn't look anything like Buster Keaton."

Leola sighed in exasperation. "I never said he did, I said he was good looking."

"Oh well, yes, he's quite attractive, I think. Is he Choctaw?"

Leola turned over the CD cover. "Says here he's Navajo and Ute."

"Wonder where the Ute's are from."

"Utah, I think."

"Well that makes sense." Lucille looked at all the gifts on the couch. "Should we wrap them separately or put them all in one big box from both of us? I can't remember who bought what, except the bow and arrows were my idea."

Just Off the Streetcar Line

"I'll remember that when the uprising starts." Leola thought for a minute. "Why don't we wrap the little ones separately so they won't get lost but put everything in one big box from both of us? I've got that box the Christmas tree came in, it'll all fit in there. You need to wrap up that dreamcatcher in some newspaper to protect it." She grabbed the "Living" section of the *Times Picayune*. "Here, use this."

Lucille examined the paper with interest. "Well look a' here. It's an article about Iron Eyes Cody. Remember him?"

Leola was pulling wrapping tissue out of the sideboard. "Yeah, I remember him, he was an actor. I think he was in a bunch of John Wayne movies."

"He was an Indian."

"Oh Lucille, John Wayne wasn't an Indian, he was Irish or something."

Lucille began wrapping up the dreamcatcher. "Not John Wayne, Iron Eyes Cody."

Leola was pulling out ribbons and bows. "No he wasn't, he was Italian. He was from down here."

"I didn't know that."

"I read it somewhere. His real name was something Italian. Don't remember what, though." Leola examined the pile of wrapping paper. "We can wrap up the little stuff in this white tissue, but the only big sheets of paper I have for that box are bright red."

"It'll have to do, then, because I don't have anything that big at my house either. We'll put some pretty bows with it, it'll be fine."

Leola stood up and grabbed her purse. "Put that stuff down; we can wrap it later. I don't know about you, but I'm hungry and I don't want to cook. How do feel about Japanese food, my treat?"

Lucille slung her bag over her arm and headed for the front door. "I'll drive. I want to get there in one piece."

"Are you insinuating that I'm a bad driver?"

"No, I'm insinuating that you have a lead foot, Mrs. Mario Andretti."

Leola locked the front door. "You know, Mario Andretti's Italian."

"I thought he was from North Carolina."

"Maybe so, but he's still Italian."

Lucille pulled out her car keys. "There are a lot of Indians in North Carolina."

"I guess so."

Just Off the Streetcar Line

"I know because Freddie and I went to a reservation up there when we went to the Smokies. I showed you the pictures."

Leola got in the passenger side of Lucille's yellow 1977 Lincoln. "I don't understand why you keep driving this road hog. You can hardly see over the steering wheel; you have to sit on the phone book just to drive."

Lucille settled in behind the wheel and carefully pulled out into the street. "I like to have plenty of steel around me."

"Well it's good thing because you hit something every time you park this old dinosaur."

"My car's in perfect condition, hardly any dents at all."

"That's because it's bigger than a Sherman tank. It's indestructible."

Lucille peered between the top of the steering wheel and the horn, then made a wide turn onto Magazine Street, narrowly missing a light pole, a trash can and a pedestrian, who quickly ran into a pizza parlor on the corner to escape death-by-Lincoln.

Leola covered her eyes and slid down into the seat. "Tell me when we get there."

*****

Mr. Charley stood naked in the open refrigerator door and viewed his prospects. Two slices of three-day-old pizza, one quarter of a muffuletta, a turkey neck, an empty jar of Blue Plate mayonnaise, a half-empty jar of Zatarain's Creole mustard, four giant dill pickles, and two six packs of Dixie beer. He grabbed the pizza and the muffuletta and put them on the table, then went back for a Dixie. The pizza went into the toaster oven, the muffuletta he stuck in the microwave. While his dinner was heating, he went back to the refrigerator for the pickles and the jar of mustard, then opened the big oven door and retrieved his underwear from the top rack. After pulling his drab and drooping drawers over his wrinkly old butt, Mr. Charley arranged his dinner on a rusty coca-cola tray he'd covered with aluminum foil, then retired to his recliner and turned on the six o'clock news.

He'd only been awake for an hour, long enough to shower and listen to the police scanner while he shaved. The scanner had revealed no activity in his neighborhood, but there had been an interesting exchange about an investigation on Euterpe Street. It seems a group of four intoxicated indigents had been barbecuing a nutria in the back yard of an abandoned house, using an old toilet as a barbecue pit and a bottle of Wild Turkey in lieu of lighter fluid. Unfortunately the flames leapt a little higher than anticipated and caught a cedar tree on fire. The fire was out, the charred nutria was removed from the toilet bowl, and one of the indigents had been taken to the drunk tank after hitting a

Just Off the Streetcar Line

policeman with the nutria carcass. His three friends had run off down Baronne Street.

Mr. Charley only watched the news on Channel 4. He had a crush on Angela Hill. He sometimes fantasized about taking her Cajun dancing at Tipitina's, then sharing a beer with her at Muddy's, maybe a burger at GB's. He was saddened at the news of her latest nuptials, but he still thought she was hot. He sighed to himself as her blond head lit up the TV screen. He hadn't had a date in ten years. He wouldn't know what to say to a woman. The thought of actually asking a woman out to dinner absolutely paralyzed him. He didn't know where he would even take a date for dinner; his culinary experience for the last ten years was mainly confined to Taco Pedro, Boudreaux's Po'boys, Tony's Tamales and Benny's Pizza Palace. If memory served him, he was pretty sure a decent date would turn up her nose at all of those fine dining establishments. He sighed and bit into the muffuletta.

The afternoon's lead story concerned the plight of Mr. Leroy Johnson, who was being loaded into a police car, and Mr. Isaiah Washington, who was cursing loudly at Mr. Johnson even as he was being lifted into an ambulance bound for Charity Hospital. Mr. Charley banged his beer bottle on the arm of his tattered recliner and threw a pickle at the TV screen as he watched Mr. Johnson being interviewed by action news reporter Lauri Plaissance.

The pretty brunette looked very young and earnest as she spoke into the microphone. "Mr.

Johnson, why did you run over Mr. Isaiah Washington?"

"He be in da way."

"But Mr. Washington was standing on the neutral ground waiting for a streetcar."

"But dat be where I was drivin' at da time."

"But why were you driving on the neutral ground?"

"It was da onliest way to get away from da *police*, who be chasin' me at da time, you see."

"Why were you being chased by the police?"

Mr. Johnson looked at the young Ms. Plaissance incredulously. "Cause dat truck be stole, lady."

Ms. Plaissance looked confused. "But where did you get the truck?"

"From da impoun' lot. I figured they's so many cars in dere, dey ain't gonna miss dat ole truck. But dey saw me comin' out da lot cause I hit da gate by accident and dragged it wif me a little ways down the street 'fo it fell off. So dey started chasin' me over by Jackson Avenue, and I just got up on da neutral ground to tries to sneak away from 'em, you see. Nobody got hurt."

"But you ran over Mr. Washington!"

Just Off the Streetcar Line

"I jes runned over his big ole feet. He be alright. We still frens."

"But he was cursing at you just now. He threatened to kill you."

"Oh, he always cussin' at me dat way. He say he gonna kill me ever time I beats him at checkers. We been knowin' each other since we was six. We bof sings in da choir by New Zion Baptist Church."

At that point a uniformed cop closed the door and the police cruiser sped off down St. Charles, leaving pretty little Ms. Plaissance standing, bewildered, on the neutral ground, thinking she should've stayed in Abbeville and married Pete Bergeron, who inherited his father's feed store. It would've been a dull life, but a sane one. "This is Lauri Plaissance for Eye Witness News."

The beautiful Angela Hill looked straight-faced into the camera and said, "Mr. Washington was taken to Charity Hospital where he is listed in stable condition. Mr. Johnson was taken to Central Lockup, where he was released on his own recognizance." Mr. Charley threw another pickle at the TV and muttered a few obscenities.

When the news was over, Mr. Charley turned off the TV and went to his bedroom to find something to wear. He was suddenly lonely and thought he might wander over to Zeke's for a beer. As he was pulling on his old fatigues, it dawned on him that he could hear drumming and chanting. He peeked out a small crack in his yellowed, dusty blinds and looked across the street at the Billiot back yard. Avery and six of his relatives were sitting around a smoking barbecue grill, banging drums and singing. He knew from experience that it would get worse as the night wore on. He remembered Lundi Gras, a few months earlier.

On Lundi Gras, the day before Mardi Gras, an uncertain number of Billiot friends and relatives had arrived from the bayou during the day to celebrate South Louisiana's biggest holiday. The cooking, singing, drumming, dancing, drinking and general revelry had spread from the Billiot back yard into the neighborhood and an impromptu block party had ensued. Mr. Charley had become sociable enough to bring a case of Dixie beer to the festivities, along with a load of shrimp from his deepfreeze. In the early evening, those who could navigate the sidewalk had walked up to St. Charles Avenue to enjoy the parade, then walked back loaded with cups and beads to rejoin the party. The cups were filled with beer and the beads were strung around wrought iron fence spikes and the necks of faux wildlife, and thrown into trees all over the neighborhood. Sometime around nine o'clock, someone set one of Mrs. Billiot's pink plastic flamingoes too close to the barbecue grill where shrimp, oysters, frog legs and alligator tails were being grilled. In trying to douse the flamingo with a Corona, Andre Dardard had set one of his braids on fire. Mr. Charley quickly drenched the flaming braid with a can of Dixie, but Andre had still gotten a little singed. It was a good

Just Off the Streetcar Line

thing he was too drunk to feel any pain. Avery had taken out his hunting knife and cut both braids the same length, then removed his cousin's shirt and applied fresh aloe to his chest. Andre passed out in one of the hammocks shortly afterward and woke up the next day wondering why his braids were shorter and half his chest hair was gone.

As Mr. Charley watched the drumming and singing across the street, he remembered that Avery was getting married tomorrow night and wondered if this was some kind of Indian bachelor party. He also wondered vaguely if they'd hired a stripper. He thought it would be a good idea to sit on his front porch for a while and see what transpired.

*****

Jackie Cheramie sat cross-legged on the living room floor, wrapping Avery's wedding gift. She knew Avery loved good coffee. He had briefly dated Lisa a couple of years ago, and Jackie remembered him talking about Hawaiian Kona, which he rarely bought because it was a whopping thirty-five dollars a pound. So Jackie had gone to a specialty coffee store in Lakeside Mall and bought a pound of Kona, along with a flamingo decanter and two large flamingo cups. She thought the flamingoes were the perfect touch, since his mother's yard was filled with them.

Jackie liked Avery; he'd always treated her like an adult, without trying to put the make on her. When he dated Lisa, Jackie had hoped the relationship would work, knowing in her heart that it would work when pigs flew south for the winter. No one as centered and stable as Avery Billiot was going to stay long with a space cadet like Lisa. Besides, everyone knew that when Avery settled down again, it would be with an Indian woman. Ever since his divorce he'd told anyone who cared to listen that he would never again tie the knot with a Dairy Queen.

Jackie had just put the gift on the coffee table when the phone rang. She looked at the caller I.D. Las Vegas. It had to be Lisa and it had to be trouble – Lisa never called if she was having a good time. Jackie sighed audibly and picked up the phone. "Hello."

It was Lisa, but she was incoherent, alternately crying and blubbering something about shooting somebody. "*Who* got shot, Lisa? Did *you* get shot?"

"No no no! It was Frank. *Frank* got shot!" More blubbering and hysterics.

"Lisa you've got to calm down. I can't understand you."

"I'm trying, I'm trying." More crying.

"Okay, Lisa, who shot Frank?"

"*I* shot him!"

"God almighty. Is he dead?"

"Hell no, he's not dead!"

"Where did you shoot him?"

Lisa was screeching, "Right here in the hotel room, dammit!" More sobbing.

"No, Lisa, I mean where on his good-for-nothin' *body* did you shoot him?"

"In the ass, I shot him in the ass," she wailed.

Jackie smiled to herself. "You shot him in the ass?"

"Yes, I *told* you that. I shot him in the ass. I just grazed him though. Does that count?"

"Depends on whether you're the one who did the shooting or the one who got shot. Now tell me how it happened."

Sniffle. "It was an accident. Sort of."

"Lisa, how did you sort of accidentally shoot him in the ass?"

Big sniffle, nose blowing. "I was aiming at his wife."

"His *wife*? Did you know he was married?"

"Well, of *course* I knew he was married."

Jackie took a deep breath. "Okay, you were aiming at his wife. Where in the name of Christ did you get a gun, Lisa?"

"It was Maureen's."

"Who's Maureen?"

"His wife. It was her gun."

Jackie closed her eyes and tried to remain calm, but her voice was understandably strained. "Where and when did all this happen, and what was his wife doing there?"

"It just happened, just now! Right here in our hotel room!" Lisa was crying again and getting hysterical.

Jackie made her voice as soothing as possible, considering the circumstances. "Okay, so that's where you are now?"

"Yeah, I'm still in the room." Crying, but less hysterical.

"Lisa, sweetie, I want you to calm down *right fucking now* and tell me exactly what happened, but *quickly*."

Shaky voice. "Maureen found out where we were and came out here. We'd just come back from the casino, and I'd just stashed my money in my suitcase, when she knocked on the door. Frank went to the door and she came in pointing a gun at him. She followed him around the room hollering at him, so I hit her over the head with my makeup case. She fell down and dropped the gun, so I grabbed it and I was aiming at her when Frank got in the way and I shot him in the ass. Sort of. I don't think I hurt him much." Lisa actually giggled. "He was trying to strangle Maureen."

"So then what happened?"

"He said, 'You bitch, you shot me!' So I got mad and shot at his other cheek. I missed though, I was way wide."

"Fuck, Lisa, this just keeps getting worse. Where is he?"

"I don't know, he ran off and she ran off after him."

A light bulb went off in Jackie's very agile brain. "Lisa, you said you were stashing your money in your suitcase. Did you win some money? I only gave you a couple hundred."

"I know, but I kept winning and winning, all over town. I've been winning for two days."

"How much, Lisa?"

"How much did I win, you mean, altogether?"

"Yes, Lisa, how much is in your suitcase?"

"Hold on." Jackie heard shuffling. "I'm counting. It's all in cash." Long pause. "I'm still counting, hold on. It's mostly in hundreds." Another long pause. Jackie heard her mother counting under her breath. "Two hundred thousand, four hundred sixty-seven and some quarters."

"Holy fuckin' *shit*, Lisa!" Jackie closed her eyes and thought for a moment. "Lisa, honey, I don't know exactly what's going on, but you sure as hell don't need to hang around there. Now you do *exactly* as I say, right now."

Sniffle. "Okay."

"Get you purse and your money. Take the money out of your suitcase right now, take all that crap out of your makeup bag and stash your money in it." Lisa's makeup bag was big enough to hold a satellite hookup. "Are you doing what I said?"

More shuffling sounds. "Yes, it's in there, all of it." She sounded shaky again.

"Where's the gun?"

"It's here on the bed."

"Wipe your prints off it and stash it somewhere now, right now, go find a place."

Just Off the Streetcar Line

"Okay, hold on." Shuffling sounds ensued, bumping, scraping. "Okay, I hid it under the hot tub, there's a space under there. I accidentally kicked it last night and the panel came off. It's hidden behind some pipes."

Jackie sighed audibly. "Is there any ID in or on your suitcase? Isn't your name on the front of it?"

"Yeah, it's in a little plastic pocket."

"Take it out, rip it up, and flush it." Jackie heard ripping and flushing. "Is there anything in your suitcase that would identify you? I know your fingerprints are all over the place, but you've never been fingerprinted before, have you?"

"No, and there's nothing in my suitcase."

"Okay, Lisa, take your makeup bag and your purse, leave your suitcase, I don't care how attached you are to those clothes, you can buy more. Now get the *fuck* outta there. I want you to go down the stairs, go out the back, walk a few blocks down the street, then get a taxi to the MGM Grand. I'm going to make you a reservation right now under my name. The name on your license is "Jaqueline Lizette Cheramie", so you can pass for me. As soon as you get to your room, you call me. This shouldn't take you more than half an hour.. Now *go!*"

"Okay, I'm going."

"Call me the minute you get to your room."

"Okay."

"Don't fuck up, Lisa." Jackie hung up the phone and immediately called the MGM Grand and made a reservation, pre-paying by credit card. Then she sat down and waited for the phone to ring.

*****

Jimmy Jackson sat on his grandmother's sofa, drinking a glass of iced tea and listening to the mellow sounds of Luther Vandross on the radio. A cool breeze ruffled the white lace curtains on the living room windows. Grandmamma was taking a nap after her big trip to Dillard's, and Jimmy was completely drained from the experience. He just wanted to rest up a little before he picked up Alice for dinner.

Jimmy was absolutely certain that he could not show his face in the Lakeside Dillard's again for quite a few years, not after today's shopping trip. Things had gone well at first; they had found the bath department without incident. Grandmamma had been looking at towels, complaining audibly about prices, but she always complained about prices. She had picked out a set of blue bath towels with matching hand towels and washcloths and was sniffing decorative soaps when trouble arrived in the form of a loud young lady who was the proud possessor of perhaps six or eight tattoos, but Jimmy could only see the uncovered parts of her body, which happened to be *most* of her body. The young lady also had purple hair and various body piercings, including three in each ear lobe, her lip, her tongue (which she stuck out at her more conservative companion, who only had pierced ears), her eyebrow and her navel.

The purple hair, piercings and tattoos were enough to cause Grandmamma to stare at the gaudy creature in total wonder and ask her if she was part of a traveling circus, but she was behaving herself. The trouble started when Grandmamma saw the girl's silver satanic ring and went into fits of apoplexy, throwing soap balls at the girl and screaming "devil child" and "get thee behind me, Satan," before finally dropping to her knees, clutching her rosary and mumbling novenas. The "devil child" started screaming obscenities at Grandma, who rose from her knees and whacked the young woman on her purple head with a blue ceramic soap dish. Two security guards arrived in time to see Jimmy pulling the little purple-haired child of Satan off a poor little old black lady cowering on the floor with her rosary. Ms. Purple Hair and her friend were escorted out of the store and a request was made that they do their shopping elsewhere in the future.

The Dillard's manager was so flustered that he apologized profusely to Grandmamma for allowing "demons from hell" in his store and gave her the towels free of charge. Grandmamma went home happy, but Jimmy was mortified. It was simply not safe to let Grandmamma outside the house, and Jimmy had no intention of letting something like this happen again.

Jimmy picked up the *Times-Picayune* from the coffee table and idly flipped through the local and national news, glancing at the headlines, before moving along to the Metro section. He loved Lolis Elie's column — always well written, always thought-provoking. Today's column was about the food of New Orleans – gumbo, red beans, oyster po'boys, softshell crabs, etoufee, jambalaya. When Jimmy finished the column, his mouth was watering and he was ready to head over to Pampy's for some fried chicken. He turned the page and glanced at the crime section. He skipped over the usual muggings and car jackings, but one little paragraph caught his attention. "Robbery, Louisiana Avenue and Freret Street. Perpetrator was a black male, approximately 30 years old, riding a child's blue bicycle. Snatched red Tazmanian Devil lunchbox from Mr. Percy Adams, age 14. Victim threw his Big Gulp at perpetrator but missed and hit the head of Mrs. Oletha Jefferson, age 72, who attacked Mr. Adams with her bag of surplus cheese. The perpetrator escaped while a melee ensued between Mr. Adams and Mrs. Jefferson." Jimmy shook his head in disgust. Now there was a perfect example of what was wrong with this city. He threw the paper in the trash and headed out the door, ready for an evening with his true love and a couple of double martinis.

*****

Rosemarie Guidry panted up her three porch steps, lugging an enormous cardboard box, a large plastic bag, and her big red canvas sack that served as a purse. She had to ease sideways through one side of the double doors; if she got any bigger, she'd have to open up the other door, which was easier than going on a diet. Rosemarie had no intention of going on a diet, anyway; she was not giving of up one morsel of food intended for her mouth.

Rosemarie plopped down on her big blue plaid sofa, dropped her things, kicked off her rubber shower thongs with the big yellow flowers, and gave a sigh of relief. Rosemarie had had a tough day. She'd gone out to Lakeside Mall to buy a wedding gift for Avery, but after much searching and clucking over the high price of retail shopping, she had finally left the mall in disgust. As she was nosing her 1972 Ford station wagon out of the back parking lot, she noticed a hardware store across the street that was going out of business, so she hopped two curbs, sideswiped a new pickup truck, and slid her aging behemoth into a parking space just big enough for a Toyota Corola. The hardware store was a gold mine. It was there that she found a musical toilet seat, a white wrought iron baker's rack, fourteen packs of light bulbs, and a ten-gallon crawfish pot. She wasn't sure what to give Avery. It was a toss-up between the musical toilet seat and the crawfish pot but, reasoning that no one could have enough crawfish pots – especially the way Avery's family entertained – Rosemarie decided on the pot, grabbed her purchases and concluded that her shopping day had come to end. She could wrap the pot in newspaper and tie green crab net string around it; she had no intention of using up an entire roll of wrapping paper on one gift when the paper would just get torn off anyway.

Rosemarie had been slowly driving down the street behind the mall, headed for home, when she noticed High End wedged between White Buffalo Books and The Jumping Java Bean. High End was the colonic clinic her friend Angela had recommended a few months ago when she was suffering from severe constipation. She said they stuck a hose up her ass and cleaned her out in about half an hour. As Rosemarie hadn't had a bowel movement in four days, she pulled into the parking lot, took up two spaces in front of a tattoo parlor, and hoped she didn't need an appointment to get hosed out.

She opened the bright blue door with a little apprehension, but High End looked just like a doctor's office, with soft gray carpet, comfortable padded black chairs, fake foliage and piped in Muzak. Olivia, the six-foot black woman behind the counter, told her that no appointment was necessary and gave her a form to fill out. Rosemarie answered all sorts of intimate questions about her eating habits and the workings of her bowels, paid up front with a credit card, then was shown to a white linoleum covered room that had a lot of faucets and gadgets mounted on the wall, a padded plastic-covered massage table with stirrups in the center of the room, a refrigerator and cabinet in the corner, and a full bathroom off to the right. Rosemarie was given a paper gown and a glass of what looked like carrot juice. She was told to drink the juice, put on the paper gown, and lay down on the table with her feet up in the stirrups. Olivia said a rectal technician would be with her in about twenty minutes, then quickly exited the room.

Rosemarie put on the little paper gown, which barely covered her two hundred and eighty pound frame, then took one sip of the juice, made a face, and poured the rest down the sink. She walked around the room, looking at all the gadgets and nozzles mounted on the wall, then slowly hefted herself up on the table and put her feet up in the stirrups. She felt exposed, vulnerable and ridiculous. She had just about decided to get off the table and go home when the door opened and a pink spaceman walked in.

He wasn't really a spaceman, of course, and wasn't a he at all but a pretty young woman named Tracey who was wearing a pink biohazard type suit, accompanied by a male midget she called Chico, who was similarly attired. Tracey explained the procedure in technical terms, then said, "Basically, we smear your butt with olive oil, stick a hose up your ass and turn the water on." Rosemarie was thinking she could've done the same thing at home with a can of Crisco and a garden hose and saved herself seventy-five bucks.

Tracey rubbed some kind of oil on Rosemarie's fifty-two inch ass, pulled a slender, clear plastic hose from the wall and slowly pushed it between Rosemarie's cheeks. After a few minutes, Tracey told the midget something was wrong because nothing was coming back out. They removed the hose and substituted it for one a little larger, but still nothing happened. Tracey adjusted the water pressure and looked quizzically at the gauges on the wall, but Rosemarie's bowels remained unmoved. After about ten minutes, Tracey pushed on Rosemarie's abdomen until she was panting inside her pink space suit, then told the midget to get up on the table and stand on Rosemarie's stomach. Chico stood on top of what he silently referred to as Mt. Everest, pressing here and there with his little feet, but Rosemarie's stomach remained hard as a rock, so he climbed back down. Finally, Tracey pulled a tube from the wall that looked like a firehose and said, "Mrs. Guidry, you must have concrete bowels. I'm afraid we're going to have to use the big hose."

With that, Rosemarie said, "Bullshit with your big hose," climbed off the table, and locked herself in the bathroom until Tracey and the midget left. She ripped off the paper gown, pulled her cotton flowered mumu over her head, grabbed her canvas bag, and rushed out of the clinic to the safety of her car. What a nightmare! She couldn't get out of Metairie fast enough. Eugenia Robichaux was right, all of Lakeside was cursed. She should've known better than to go out there.

Having escaped the colonic horrors of High End, Rosemarie decided to console herself with a little snack before dinner. She lumbered back to the kitchen, poured herself a Barq's rootbeer, then sliced off an end of a loaf of French bread, mashed down the spongy middle and poured condensed milk in the center. She was just polishing off her appetizer and draining the last of the Barq's when it hit. Rosemarie felt a rumbling and a pressure deep within her bowels, like a subway barreling through the earth. She ran for the bathroom and sat down on the pink toilet seat just as four day's worth of backed up debris finally exited the tunnel with a rush.

*****

Miss Libby turned out her front room light and peeked out of a sliver in the drapes. Mr. Charley was still sitting out on his porch drinking beer, waiting hopefully for naked girls to appear in Avery's backyard. Through her open window Miss Libby could hear Avery's cousins beating a big drum and singing something about a gator woman with a lethal tail. That nonsense would go on until eleven o'clock tonight, when the Yankee lady would run over in her bathrobe and scream at them, which would just make them sing louder to drown her out. She would jump up and down and holler and call them a bunch of drunken savages; the cousins would spray her with beer and throw crawfish at her, then they would make up songs about her. At that point Marsha would run screaming into her house, covered with beer and crawfish juice, and call the police, who would eventually come and break things up around midnight, if they showed up at all. It depended on who was being shot, knifed or carjacked across town. The police had their hands full on the weekends; hysterical women screaming about drums and beer and crawfish were a very low priority. Miss

Libby figured she could slip away down the street during all the commotion.

She went to the kitchen in the back of the house and looked at the hedge clippers standing up against the refrigerator. She'd cleaned and oiled them, then sharpened the blades with her dead husband's whetstone; they were ready for action. The clippers couldn't perform with the speed of the weed eater, but they could do the job efficiently. Miss Libby knew there were some ragged looking banana trees over on Camp Street that desperately needed the attention of a gardener. And she'd noticed a rose bush around the corner that was running wild across the sidewalk. She was sure she could find a number of projects during her evening sojourn.

Miss Libby mentally worked out her route while heating up a can of vegetable soup. She never had been much of a cook and figured she was too old to take up the culinary arts now. In fact, she wasn't interested in much of anything anymore. When Jeremy was alive she used to enjoy going out to the cemeteries with him. For forty years Jeremy made a good living as a cemetery plot salesman, a job he seemed to truly enjoy. He was also an incurable romantic, always bringing her flowers. She knew he stole them from funeral sprays, but she never let on that she knew. Besides, she rationalized, better that the flowers be enjoyed by the living than ignored by the dead.

More than anything else, Miss Libby had enjoyed going to the wakes. There was always a lot of free food and she got a kick out of standing around listening to gossip about the deceased. A few times fights broke out. She remembered one funeral in particular, where the widow was confronted by her dead husband's mistress. The widow wound up with crawfish dangling from her veil, and the mistress went home wearing most of a strawberry shortcake. A little excitement in an otherwise dull day. But the most exciting funeral she ever attended was the time a widow set her dead husband's crotch on fire during the viewing, screaming, "Let's have a weenie roast, Harold!" The priest doused the flames with the bowl of holy water, but not before the fire had devoured what were once Harold's private parts, leaving a smoldering, blackened hole in the middle of the casket. The priest calmly placed a small bouquet of gardenias in the missing section of Harold's anatomy and the viewing continued.

Jeremy had been a top salesman, and over the years he had won, among other things, a new Buick, a ski boat, a small fishing camp at Lake Bourne, and lavish trips to New York, Walt Disney World in Orlando, Bimini, San Francisco, Acapulco and Hawaii. His success as a salesman was due to one simple trick: he told everyone what they wanted to hear. Depending on his clientele, people were told they would be buried on sacred Indian burial grounds or on the very spot where Jean Lafitte was secretly laid to rest or where Napoleon was originally supposed to be buried or whatever other lie would suffice. Jeremy always psyched out his customers by observing them in their homes and with a few simple questions. The deeply religious might be told that the crypt he had in mind for them had been the exact location of a Madonna sighting thirty years ago. Then he would cross himself and utter a prayer. Whatever worked. Jeremy knew his city and its history, knew its people and their idiosyncrasies. He was a born salesman. He was also a wonderful husband and father, and Miss Libby sorely missed him.

Jeremy had died of a heart attack while screaming obscenities at the Saints when they lost a home game. Miss Libby always said he died of apoplexy. She thought of suing the Saints – after all, her husband had died because they were a lousy football team – but didn't have the stomach for the years of litigation. She also thought of asking Miss Beulah to put a voodoo curse on the football team, but upon further reflection she decided someone had done that a long time ago, so she dropped the whole thing and took up the topiary arts instead. The only other thing she enjoyed doing was putting together jigsaw puzzles and watching TV. Since she had a few hours to kill, she flipped channels until she found an "Andy Griffith Show" marathon, then sat down with her soup and iced tea at the dining room table, where she was working on a picture puzzle of the gardens at the Palace of Versailles.

*****

Graham sat on his balcony in the French Quarter, sipping a glass of Austrian white wine and watching the ex-circus dwarves in the apartment across the street make mad passionate love in their dining room. They always left the blinds up and the lights on. Tonight Lorenzo was wearing a pink tutu, a black Lone Ranger mask and lime green combat boots. His wife, Freda, looked splendid in her topless ringmaster outfit, complete with suspenders, tophat and crotchless tuxedo pants. At the moment they were christening the dining room table, but only moments ago Freda had literally swung upside down from the brass chandelier while giving Lorenzo a blow job. They were a nimble couple. Graham decided to go inside when Freda strapped a dildo contraption to her nose. Some things should be done completely in private.

Graham wandered into his own dining room, where he found Isabella sitting on a bar stool, adjusting Victor's angel wings. She was naked save a pair of red Prada sandals and a black thong. Victor looked stunning in a white chiffon cocktail dress and rhinestone dog collar; the little gold and white angel wings flaring from the shoulder pads were especially fetching. Isabella added one of her long blonde wigs and a little tiara. "Behold!" she announced. "Mimi is born."

"You look more like Fabio in drag," snickered Graham, pulling the champagne bottle from the ice bucket. "Jeez, you guys drank almost a whole magnum!"

Victor giggled. "We're just a teensy bit tipsy." He rose elegantly from the Chippendale dining chair and promptly fell off his size twelve gold platform

Just Off the Streetcar Line

sandals. Graham pulled him up into a standing position and helped him readjust his wings and falsies. "I may need a little help with the stairs," he hiccupped, throwing a white ostrich feather boa around his neck.

Isabella bent over the dining room table and dipped one of her beautiful breasts into a champagne glass, then strutted like a long-legged cat into the master bedroom, lowered herself onto the lap of her current girlfriend Julia, who was sitting on the dressing table bench in a pink silk shirt and red tie, and stuck the champagne soaked nipple into Julia's mouth. While they nuzzled each other, Victor looked at the champagne glass. "I'd dip Mr. Winky in there, but he's all tied up."

Graham downed the last of the champagne. "Don't try it, pal, it burns. I was being similarly playful one Halloween night a few years ago. Spent the next hour with my pecker stuck in the ice bucket. There I was, in a pointy-eared mask and a Batman cape, with my dick on ice. Good way to lose a hardon for the rest of the night."

As the scene in the bedroom escalated to the moan-and-tussle stage, Graham decided he was hungry. "We're having dinner in an hour," Victor reminded him."

"Which means we don't eat for maybe an hour and a half. Besides, there's chocolate cherry cheesecake in the fridge."

Victor teetered into the kitchen as fast as the gold platforms would allow. "You're on, girlfriend."

Forty minutes later Isabella emerged from the bedroom in a slinky red sequined gown, her makeup perfect and every hair in place. Julia trailed behind her in a pink pants suit and matching fedora. Isabella said Julia went in for the soft butch look; Graham thought she looked like Little Richard.

Victor grabbed his evening bag, a little white and blue beaded thing made to look like a swan. "I guess we're all ready," he trilled. As his winged and feathered friend half slid, half stumbled down the spiral staircase, Graham wondered if Irene's was ready for them. He furtively crossed himself and hoped for the best.

*****

Mr. Charley watched the Billiot house from his porch until after dark, but no strippers appeared, just more Billiots and Dardards. When they broke out the beer and lit the barbecue grills, Mr. Charley decided to become sociable. He retrieved two six packs of Dixie longnecks from his house, along with a sizable sack of frogs from last night's foray at Shell Beach and a quart jar of turtle meat he'd picked up at a bait shop that morning. He really didn't cook anyway, and he suddenly wanted to be a part of what he knew would be more than twenty-four hours of wedding festivities. Truthfully, Mr. Charley was just tired of being so damned lonely.

He crossed the street with his goodies, which he presented to Livonia, who was a little surprised at this burst of neighborliness. When she said, "Why thank you, Charley," and kissed him on the cheek, he noticed how pretty she was in her blue dress and her braids all wrapped around her head. Why had he never noticed before that Livonia was such an attractive woman? Charley was suddenly gripped with an attack of shyness. He mumbled congratulations on her son's impending nuptials and hurried out the back door with his beer, which was enthusiastically received by the cousins and added to the ice and beer-filled wading pool in the back yard. He sat down on a wooden bench next to Avery, who had been elected to shuck oysters since he had big strong hands and he was sober. Mr. Charley grabbed an oyster knife and began popping open the tough slate shells. They sat in silence for a while, throwing the little gray bodies into the silver washtub.

"How you doin' these days, Charley?" Avery asked without looking up.

"Could be better." Charley threw a shell in the trash can and grabbed another from the sack.

"What's the matter? I know you ain't sick."

"Naw, I ain't sick."

"You're a lonesome old coot, Charley. Admit it." Avery threw out the empties and grabbed a few more from the sack. "Can't do nothing about bein' old, but you don't have to be lonely."

Just Off the Streetcar Line

Charley winced a little as he pried open a big one. "Arthritis."

Avery grunted. "Me too."

Charley looked steadily at his shell. "Your mama sure looks purty tonight."

Avery grinned and chuckled a little. "You just now noticed? My mama's always been pretty. You been livin' in a deep freeze."

Charley sighed. "Yeah, I guess so." He peered into the sack. Only a handful left. He grabbed an oyster and cleared his throat. "I don't guess she'd ever go to Luther's Barbecue with an old sorry asshole like me, huh?"

Avery emptied the sack. "You ever ask her?"

"Well no."

"Why not?"

Charley gulped his beer. "Just figured I got nothin' to offer a woman. Haven't been on a date in so long, I wouldn't know what to do."

"How long?"

Charley thought a minute. "Little Bush's daddy was president."

Avery laughed and slapped Charley on the back. "Jesus, Charley, your pecker's probably petrified by now!"

Charley just blinked at him. "Sad, huh?"

Avery gave him a sidelong glance. "What's sad, bro', is your wardrobe. The bums in Lafayette Park look more elegant that you do." Avery pitched another little gray blob into the tub. "You don't have to live like this, you know. Does that thang still work?"

"Huh?"

"Your pecker, dude, does it still work or is it extinct?"

"I think it still has some life to it; I haven't taken it for a ride in a while, though."

Avery tossed the last of the shells into the big purple trash can and grinned at Charley. "My mama likes wrestling."

Charley was rinsing his hands in a bowl of lemon water. "What do you mean?"

"I mean she likes wrestling, especially mud wrestling. And hockey — she likes to watch 'em fight. Last hockey game she went to, she said it was boring, not enough action. She's only happy when they whack each other with the hockey sticks or somebody gets hit with a puck. Pass me that bowl when you finish."

Just Off the Streetcar Line

Charley grinned for the first time in a week. "Not too many women are fond of raslin' and hockey."

Avery pointed at a big, square woman with long gray braids laughing with a group of old men drinking Turbo Dog beer. "You see that big old woman over there the size of a rhinoceros? That's my mama's sister Philomena. When she was younger she used to wrestle gators down in the marsh, made a good living at it. Her husband made her stop when a gator took off part of her left hand and she couldn't get a good enough grip no more. She went back to runnin' cock fights after that."

Charley wiped his mouth on the back of his sleeve. "These ain't delicate people, are they, son?"

Avery laughed. "No siree. That's why my mama came to town, to escape that kind of life. She was born in a chickee, you know, a palmetto hut. Lived a long time on a houseboat down in Isle Jean Charles. They fished and trapped, hunted and farmed. Life was awful hard for Indians in the marsh back then. Terrible prejudice and poverty, you just have no idea."

"How did they make it?"

"Same way they always made it, before white people showed up and destroyed their way of life. They worked hard and took care of each other and they never gave up."

Charley looked at Philomena in awe. "Never met a lady wrestler before, much less one who wrestled alligators." He grabbed another Dixie from the icy wading pool. "How'd your folks end up here?"

Avery grabbed a can of Barq's and popped the top. "My old man had been asking my mama to marry him since they were six years old. When she was eighteen she finally told him if he'd run off to New Orleans with her, she'd marry him. She told me she wanted to marry him anyway, but it was a good way to get him to take her away from the bayou. So they ran off to the big city and my old man became a butcher, finally opened up that shop over on Freret Street. You remember it." Charley nodded. "Mama never did learn how to drive, though, even after they came up here. Her pa never had a car. When he used to come up to visit, he would take his pirogue up to the road and wait until he could catch a ride to Houma, and from there he caught the bus to New Orleans. When he got here he had to find a cab driver who spoke French, because he didn't speak no English."

"How come he didn't just call your dad when he got to town and ask him to pick him up at the bus station?"

Avery laughed. "Didn't know how to use the phone, never did learn how until he was old and came to live with us the last few years of his life, after the oil company stole his land."

"They stole his land?! How could they do that?"

"Because they're big and they're evil and they do shit like that, Charley. When his brother and nephew hired a lawyer and started a lawsuit, my grandpa told them they ought to drop it or they'd wind up face down in the marsh, which is exactly what happened. That's when my grandpa came to live with us. He was a traittor, like me, a medicine person." Avery grinned at Charley, who looked a little overwhelmed by all this information. "You like butterscotch cake, Charley?"

"Huh? Uh, yeah, I sure do, why?"

Avery slapped him on the back and turned him toward the back door. "Because my mama's comin' out the back door with a butterscotch pound cake right this very minute. She won't mind if you cut you a piece. Go on — she hardly ever bites." Avery propelled Charley in Livonia's direction, then walked over to the gate to help his cousin T-Roy, who was trying to drag an entire dead deer by its horns through the narrow opening.

*****

Marsha Fellows lay in the twin bed listening to her raucous neighbors thumping a drum and singing something about Bucktown girls. She had no idea who Bucktown girls were, but it sounded like they had a lively social life. Those wild Indians over there had been carrying on like that since before sunset, doing God knows what, *eating* God knows what – she heard them earlier shouting something about "cookin' dis here nutria da right way, bro', you got to skin it firs', you gonna stink up dis whole side 'a town!" She knew what a nutria was, she'd seen one on the Discovery channel – it was a big swamp rat, that's all it was. Those awful people were eating swamp rats and alligator and heaven knows what else, probably snakes. Those swamp people would eat anything that crawled, slithered, flew or swam. Well she was getting out of this insane asylum tomorrow morning; she'd decided she couldn't wait until Monday. The car was packed and ready to roll. She hadn't heard from Graham in two days and knew in her heart he had already left her. She didn't know where he was but he wasn't coming home and she no longer cared.

Marsha was so tightly wound she couldn't sleep anyway, and the noise outside was getting worse. She wanted very badly to call the police, but she knew from past experience that it wouldn't do any good at all. That awful Indian man next door was related to half the cops in town. Seemed like everybody in the *state* was related – Louisiana had to be the most incestuous place she had ever seen in her life.

She threw the sheet off and went to the front window, just in time to see some type of police vehicle pull up onto the sidewalk. Well thank God somebody else had sense enough to call the police, she thought. Her glee was short-lived, though. She saw two plainclothes officers exit the car and go around to the back and pop open the trunk. Just as she was wondering what kind of weapons were stashed back there, she saw them tugging on something big and bulky. One man yelled, "Hey cuz, we need some help over here," and they were immediately joined by two scruffy looking men in braids, one who actually had feathers stuck in his hair and some kind of blue face paint. They were obviously drunk. For a moment Marsha's heart stopped and she had visions of a war party, especially when the drumming started again. Then one of the officers said, "Whatchou got up for, Cooney, Mardi Gras? Your makeup's worse than my wife's." They all laughed and he said, "Here, grab the feet, cuz; this here pig ain't light." That's when Marsha noticed they were trying to pull an enormous pig out of the trunk. So much for the police coming to her aid.

Marsha went downstairs to the kitchen and lit a fire under the tea kettle. A cup of tea was one of the few things she could cook without creating a pile of toxic waste. And her failures in the culinary arts were not limited to the Cajun cooking disaster of a few nights ago. No, Marsha's ineptitude in the kitchen extended to the global culinary community — she had mangled recipes from France, Italy, Greece, China, Japan, Lebanon, Mexico and Germany. If there was such a thing as a chef's hit list, Marsha was at the top of its most-wanted. Graham had recently told her to do the world a favor and limit her cooking activities to cold cereal and carry-out. Poor Marsha, she really had tried, but her heart was never in it. She had attempted to cook spicy, exotic food that she loathed and the disastrous results were to be expected. And of course she had no talent for cooking or anything else creative. Marsha was a dull person whose favorite meal was roast beef with mashed potatoes and green peas. "Truck driver food," Graham had sneered. When she had asked what was so bad about good old solid, American food, Graham had replied, "It's boring, Marsha, just like you," and had slammed out of the house. For the last fifteen years they had eaten together only a couple of nights a week at best anyway, and that was only when Graham wasn't traveling. In truth, Marsha had seen little of her husband the past fifteen years. And when he was home, Graham preferred exotic, delicate dishes rather than tough, stringy roast beef; he also preferred to eat out, and he definitely preferred anyone else's company to Marsha's.

The longer Marsha sat in her kitchen and thought about her loveless marriage, the madder she got. Her anger was fueled with sips of tea laced with peppermint schnapps. She finally slammed her fist on the table and said, "Fuck you, Graham." She had made a decision. She'd get dressed and leave tonight. And since she was leaving everything in the house to Graham, why should it be left undamaged? Marsha was now a woman with a mission. She ran upstairs, dressed quickly and left her two suitcases by the door. Then she went through the house, plugging bathtub drains, sink drains, and the kitchen sink, leaving the cold water running all over the house. She also left a big "FUCK YOU, I'M GONE!!" in pink lipstick on the bedroom mirror. But Marsha made a mistake — she neglected to plug up the front, back and side doors to the old camelback house, and like most old houses in New Orleans, those doors had a good inch or two between

Just Off the Streetcar Line

the bottom of the door and the floor. If you want to successfully flood a house, you have to plug up the holes.

*****

Jackie Cheramie was watching CNN when the phone rang shrilly next to the computer. She lunged at it from across the room, knocking over her glass of chardonnay and a bust of Napoleon wearing Mardi Gras beads. "Yeah?"

"Okay, baby, I'm here." A little sniffle.

"You're at the Grand, Lisa?"

"Yeah." She started to cry again.

"Don't get wacko on me again. What's your room number? 2207. Okay, Lisa, you stay put, order braised rattlesnake from room service, drink up everything in the little bar, I don't care, but don't you *dare* leave that room, you hear me? I'm coming to get you. I'll be there first thing in the morning."

"Okay." Crying harder now.

Jackie hung up and sat at her computer for a moment to decide on a plan of action. Jackie did very little on impulse; she was rational and methodical and endowed with an IQ of a hundred and eighty-three. If there was any trouble at all, she would need backup. She thought about Avery, but she couldn't ask him to come with her — he was getting married in less than twenty-four hours. He would accompany her to Las Vegas if she asked, but she just couldn't impose, not under the circumstances.

Avery had helped Jackie once before, two years ago, when Lisa had called Jackie from a French Quarter hotel room, absolutely hysterical. When Jackie and Avery arrived thirty minutes later, what they found left Jackie shaken for months — Lisa's face was a mass of bruises, she had a busted lip and a concussion, a broken rib and a broken arm. She had also been raped so violently that her genitals were torn and bleeding — there was blood all over the bed and the carpet. Jackie sat down on the other bed in utter shock while Avery called his cousin, Adrian, who was assigned to the Sixth District police station at the time. Eight minutes later Adrian arrived with his partner, Desiree, who took one look at Lisa and threw up in the trashcan. Adrian muttered "Gawd almighty" and called the paramedics. Before she was taken to Charity Hospital, Lisa told Adrian she had been attacked by a tourist named Keith Brody from Jackson, Mississippi — she knew that was his true identity because she had sneaked a peek at his driver's license while he was in the bathroom, before he became violent. When Jackie asked Adrian if she thought they would catch him and put him in jail, Adrian just looked at Avery, who said, "Don't you worry about it, baby, it'll be taken care of." Two days later Mr. Brody's car was discovered abandoned at the Mississippi Welcome Station just the other side of the Louisiana state line. A week after that, Mr. Brody's body was found floating face down in Bayou Teche; he appeared to have died from choking on his own genitals, which had been severed from their original position and shoved down his throat. The case remains unsolved.

Upon reflection, Jackie decided there was only one other person to call.

*****

Louie was wide awake drinking Abita beer and watching Yogi and Booboo on the Cartoon Network when the phone rang.

"Louie?"

"Yeah?"

"You doin' anything right this minute?"

Sexy female voice, couldn't place it. "Not a goddamned thing I couldn't give up for a booty call. Who is this?"

Soft little laugh. "It's Jackie, and I wish this were a booty call, but actually I'm a damsel in distress."

"Well hell, darlin', that's my specialty. What's up?"

"Could you go out to Las Vegas with me, like right away? My nickel, of course."

"Well sure, I'll go out to Vegas with you, but you'll never get a plane out at this hour."

That's what Jackie liked about Louie, no questions, no hesitation. "I know, but there's a flight out at eight thirty-five in the morning," she said, "I checked."

"I'll be over at six thirty. Get some sleep."

"Okay, Louie, thanks, *big* thanks."

"No problem, babe. Uh, Jackie?"

"Yeah?"

"You wanna fill me in a little?"

Jackie sighed. "It's Lisa, she's in a little trouble again."

"Big surprise. Is she in jail?"

"No, she's at the MGM Grand."

Louie took a swig of Abita. "Well, that makes it easier."

Jackie yawned. "I'll give you rest of the story in the morning. And I'll pay you your regular rate, of course."

"I don't want you to pay me."

"I insist on paying you."

"Well in that case it'll cost you one pair of black panties."

"Black panties?"

"That's my price."

"Sold."

They hung up and Louie turned off the TV, set his alarm clock and went to bed. Then he lay in the dark and thought about the last time he'd helped Jackie rescue Lisa from herself.

After Lisa had been beaten and raped in the Quarter, she had lain low for a while, went to an expensive spa out in southern California — Rancho something-or-other — and stayed away from men for months. Then a year ago she and her girlfriend Mitzi, who was even dingier than Lisa, decided to take a three-week Caribbean cruise. Ten days later, Jackie got a call from Venezuelan authorities telling her not to worry, that her sister and her friend had been found wandering down a dirt road and they were safe, the only problem being that Lisa had amnesia. Jackie, who had just returned from five days in Lake Tahoe with a race car driver named Marco, had not even listened to her phone messages yet and had no idea what they were talking about. The Venezuelan cop told her that when Mitzi and Lisa had gone ashore in Caracas they had been abducted a few hours later by rebels who dumped them into canvas sacks, threw them in the back of a pickup truck, and took off up into the hills. Fortunately for Lisa and Mitzi, the truck's tailgate popped open when the truck hit a pothole and the two women rolled out of the back of the truck and into a ditch. They extricated themselves from the canvas sacks and were picked up a little while later by a farmer on his way to Caracas, but unfortunately Lisa had suffered a blow to her head when they fell off the truck and she had amnesia. However, the Venezuelan authorities could not keep them and the two women were now back on the cruise ship, headed for Mexico. Jackie was unable to get through to the ship due to bad weather, so she waited to hear from somebody, anybody who could tell her something about her mother's condition.

Three days later Mitzi called to tell Jackie that Lisa was holed up in a hotel in Cancun with a bullfighter; she still had amnesia and she wouldn't get back on the ship. Mitzi told Jackie to come down there and collect her mother herself, she had to reboard the ship soon and she'd had enough of Lisa and this whole insane trip. Jackie had shown up on Louie's doorstep at four in the morning with Lisa's latest tale of woe. Louie told her that no seventeen year old girl was going off to Mexico alone to rescue her thoroughly fucked up mother from some bullfighter, so he accompanied Jackie to Cancun on the eleven-thirty plane. By the time they found Lisa she was alone in her hotel room, her memory restored. She had gotten loaded the night before, passed out in the bathroom and bumped her head; when she came to she had her memory back but no memory of the bullfighter, whom she threw out of her room. The three of them stayed in Cancun for five days. Lisa took up with a Mariachi singer from the hotel, and Louie wound up in bed with Jackie one afternoon after a swim. He resisted for five minutes, on the grounds that Jackie was only seventeen. When she reminded him that they were in Mexico, a long way from U.S. puritanical moral codes, it took him ten seconds flat to remove her wet bikini.

Louie stared at his ceiling fan and tried to go to sleep in spite of his tremendous hardon.

*****

Dave Richard and his aunt, Minnie Landry, were standing in line at Dave's favorite coffeehouse, discussing the movie they'd just seen. Once a month, when Judy attended her Women in Business meetings (which Dave knew were thinly-veiled male bashing meetings where some poor sucker was always barbecued in effigy based solely on his unfortunate gender), Dave took his eighty-year-old Aunt Minnie to dinner and a movie. He had to choose the restaurant and movie carefully due to Aunt Minnie's delicate constitution (absolutely everything gave her heartburn) and her aversion to sex or violence in movies, which left out almost everything but Walt Disney. Dave favored action movies – Steven Segal, Arnold Schwartzenegger, Bruce Willis, Clint Eastwood – but he could also appreciate a good drama. Judy loved all those romantic movies, which he usually hated and which she refused to take him to see; she said he wiggled through every love scene and snorted at the dialogue. To keep the peace they usually rented movies and watched them separately. Tonight Dave had taken Aunt Minnie to see *A Beautiful Mind*, which Aunt Minnie loved but gave Dave the creeps. He walked out of the theater poking at his mystified aunt, who said what the hell are you doing? "Just checking," said Dave. When she asked what he was checking for, he said he just wanted to make sure she was really there. She said well if he was crazy he wouldn't know the difference, would he, so just cut it out.

Dave was still thinking about the movie as they stood in line and had just ordered their beverages when suddenly there was a commotion behind them. Dave turned around and saw a chubby, geeky little middle-aged man with a bad haircut rushing toward the counter, clad in nothing but a pair of white briefs. "Underwear party!" shouted the geek. "Underwear party! Everybody come to the underwear party!" Then he wandered over to the tables against the wall and invited several customers to his underwear party. This being New Orleans, no one was either surprised or offended at the unattractive geek in briefs; they all just blew him off and went back to their laptops.

Oh great, thought Dave, the one time I bring my eighty-year-old aunt in here for coffee, we're accosted by Super Geek in his underwear. Behind him, a man who looked like Robert Dinero sighed and leaned against the pastry case. "Not again," he muttered.

"Somebody forgot to take his medication." Dinero pulled out his cell phone and punched in a number. "Hey Herman, your brother's over here at PJ's in his underwear inviting everybody to a party. You wanna come get him?" He listened for a minute and said, "How should I know what he's doin' over here. Maybe Starbucks threw him out again." Another pause. "No, he's not wearing the black thong this time, they're just regular white Fruit of the Loom. But he's not pretty, Herman; he looks like the Pilsbury doughboy in drawers." Dinero hung up and put in his order for coffee.

A few minutes later, as Dave was trying to pay for their drinks, Super Geek came back to the counter and invited a speechless Aunt Minnie and Dave to his party. At that point, Sarah, the cashier, had had enough. "Sir, you can't come in here with no clothes on!" she scolded. Super Geek looked genuinely hurt and said, meekly, "Okay," and calmly walked to the front of the shop and sat down at a table full of fifteen-year-old girls wearing Uptown Girls Soccer Team shirts. As they sat giggling at the Pilsbury Doughboy, Dinero looked around and muttered, "Oh God, there's a lawsuit waiting to happen." He casually sauntered over to the Doughboy and invited him to sit with him at a table back in the corner.

The only available table was right next to Dinero and the Doughboy, but at least it was a table by the window. Dave loved sitting by the window and watching all the coeds walk by in short-shorts, miniskirts and halter tops; it was one of life's little pleasures. They had just sat down when the Doughboy decided to stand on the shaky little table and break out into song, specifically "I Love Being a Girl." He was doing little kicks when Aunt Minnie started to giggle; by the time Dinero pulled Doughboy off the table, she was in full-blown laughter, the tears rolling down her cheeks. Dinero took off his shirt and made Doughboy put it on, then hustled him out of the coffeehouse, presumably to await Herman's arrival.

Dave patted Aunt Minnie on the arm. "I am so sorry about this, Aunt Minnie," he said.

Aunt Minnie took deep breaths and wiped her eyes with a napkin. "Why are you sorry, David? This is the most fun I've had in years!" She looked out the window and saw Doughboy doing the can-can on the sidewalk, which started her howling again. Oh Lord, thought Dave, I'll never hear the end of the this!

*****

Eugenia Robichaux sat on her couch in her second parlor, absently scratching Tigger's ears. Tigger was on his back, splayed out on the couch, alternately grunting in his sleep and passing wind. Occasionally Eugenia sprayed gardenia air freshener in the direction of Tigger's tail, commenting on the condition of his bowels. "Who-eee, Tigger! I shouldn't a' never give you them red beans and ham hocks for your dinner, boy. You got some powerful gas in your innerds. We bottle up that stuff, we could make some money, sell your evil wind to the gov'ment as a secret weapon."

Michel had not returned from the bayou, so Eugenia knew he was spending the night with Uncle Armand. Eugenia was sitting up in her yellow cotton nightgown way past her bedtime because she was suffering from simultaneous indigestion and constipation and couldn't sleep. After a couple of hours of discomfort, which she tried to ignore while watching an Andy Griffith marathon on TV Land, she had finally given in and drunk a white clay and coconut oil mixture, and she was now waiting for it to pass through her system. She couldn't have slept much anyway, what with all that commotion going on next door. Right now a sizable group of Avery's guests were singing along to a Dr. John CD turned up full blast. Not really singing in Eugenia's opinion, more like howling, some song about Mama Rue and the queen of the little red, white and blue.

Eugenia had watched the Yankee lady load up her car all day. At first she thought maybe she was going on a trip, but she had filled her car with so much stuff, Eugenia figured she was probably leaving her husband. She didn't see a moving van, though, so Marsha was traveling light. She wondered if Marsha's husband had already left. Not that it mattered much — he was never at home anyway. Eugenia had figured out that he spent *maybe* two nights a week at the house next door, a fact that she discussed in some length with Tigger.

"That man ain't never home, Tigger. Nobody travels that much, not even my second cousin Roland who used to stay down at Pointe-aux-Chienes by his Mama house when he was shrimping and over by his wife and kids at Larose the rest of the time. That man loved Marie — he was home every minute he could be, making more babies. That poor woman give him nine babies, Tigger. I'm glad you fixed, boy, not spreadin' it around the neighborhood. But he had to be out on the boat sometimes for weeks at a time, and then he and Dickie Plaissance had to run it to market all over the place. They had crab pots, too, and he and Dickie used to go out sharkin' sometimes, but mostly they shrimped. Dickie went off to the Pacific fishin' one year when he was young, but he didn't like bein' away from home and bein' out in the cold like that, so he come home. He worked at that poagie plant for a while, but he hated that — said it smelled like Satan's butt in there. Poagie does stink, Tigger, worse than all the gas in your old bad self. So that's when Dickie talked Roland into going into the shrimping business with him." She paused to spray gardenia in the direction of Tigger's hind quarters. "But they was out on a boat and traveling around tryin' to sell they shrimp. That man next door ain't nothin' but a college professor, got no reason to be away from home all the time 'less he wants to. No, Tigger, that man got him a woman somewhere else he lives with most of the time. Not that I blame him, Tigger — his wife's cookin' would drive away Jesus himself." Tigger responded with another mild explosion from the depths of his bowels.

Sometime during the Andy Griffith marathon, Eugenia saw Marsha run out of the house with a couple of suitcases, throw them in the car and screech off down the street. Eugenia turned to Tigger and said, "There she goes, Tigger. She leavin', son. Bet she ain't comin' back. And good riddance." Tigger just scratched his fleas in reply. Marsha had been rather unpopular in the neighborhood, but Tigger had primarily ignored her, as he ignored most humans. His only experience with Marsha had been one morning when his high-strung next door neighbor had come outside looking for her newspaper, which just happened to have been thrown under the banana tree where Tigger lay sleeping peacefully. Marsha had reached under the enormous banana frond, bitching and cursing about the stupid paperboy who had missed her porch for the four hundredth time for fucking crissakes, the little son of a bitch just didn't give a shit, nobody in this godforsaken town had the good sense or the goddamned drive to hit a lick at a snake, much less aim properly at the porch. Marsha ferociously snatched the newspaper, swatting Tigger's nose in the process. Tigger jumped up with a start, sneezing and whining and puffing his offended nose. The startled Marsha screamed bloody murder and ran into her house, slamming the door behind her. Tigger blinked a few times, scratched his stomach with his hind leg, circled the banana tree twice, then settled back down with a grunt to resume his early morning snooze.

Eugenia was nodding out on the couch, still holding the can of gardenia spray, when nature called.

The cousins next door were doing a rousing, albeit drunken, rendition of "She Came in Through the Bathroom Window" and Tigger was snoring when the white clay laxative hit home. Eugenia jumped up, rolling Tigger off the couch, and ran for the bathroom, hollering, "Hold it, together, cheeks, hold it together!" Tigger sat up a little dazed, shook his head a couple of times and sneezed, then passed out on the floor, Eugenia's bowel predicament hardly creating a ripple in his little world.

*****

Donnie Lee pulled up in front of his house and carefully parked on the front lawn. He didn't think he was all *that* drunk, but he'd had a few cosmos at Cowpokes with the boys and he wasn't taking any chances with his precious little sports car. He'd driven home very, very carefully at a top speed of twenty-five miles an hour; he didn't want to alert the police to his condition. He wasn't sure how he'd gotten out of the Quarter — his memory was just a wee bit fuzzy on details. He did, however, remember that things had gotten a little rowdy at Cowpokes. He remembered riding the mechanical bull with somebody, and he remembered being naked, but for the life of him he couldn't remember who the other rider had been — no name or face came to mind at all. He remembered the cheering crowd, so he must have performed well. Oh lord, those cosmos were lethal!

Just Off the Streetcar Line

Donnie Lee was willing himself to let go of the steering wheel and get out of the car — very slowly, of course, no need to be hasty — when he noticed little rope bracelets dangling from his wrists. Now where the hell did those come from? He searched his vodka-fogged brain and a picture started to form, a picture of Donnie Lee, tied to a rail, jeans down around his ankles, being spanked. He couldn't remember who the spanker was or if it was before or after the bull riding incident, but he remembered someone in the crowd yelling something about bad boys. It must have been a good night, he must have had fun, but the details eluded him just right now.

Donnie Lee noticed that the Indians across the street were celebrating the upcoming nuptials in grand style — there were drunk people everywhere, spilling from the backyard into the street. There was cooking, there was drinking, there was ... a live pig? Surely Donnie Lee was hallucinating; nobody kept a live pig in the city, at least not in this neighborhood. Not lately, anyway, not since Bubba Breaux had moved out to Gentilly. Bubba had kept a pet pig named Lover in his back yard, along with a laying hen named Doodoo and a big turtle named Axel that swam around in a little plastic swimming pool. Unfortunately, Axel bit Doodoo's head off one morning in a fit of pique after Doodoo charged the normally placid tortoise, pecking and squawking. Bubba ran outside to find feathers scattered everywhere and Doodoo's head laying in a pool of blood and pig excrement, and Axel munching peacefully on Bubba's lettuce growing under the mulberry tree. The frightened Lover was hiding under the house, squeaking pitifully. Bubba cried for poor little Doodoo and buried him under a crepe myrtle tree. Soon afterward he gave away Axel to the zoo and moved with Lover out by Dillard University.

Donnie Lee inched a little closer to the street and squinted at Avery's garage wall, not sure about what he was seeing. "Holy shit," he squeaked. "It's Bambi!" And Bambi didn't look so hot. Actually, Bambi was hanging on the outside wall of the garage by his horns, dead as a doornail. Donnie Lee stumbled across the street, tears rolling down his face. "Bambi! Somebody shot Bambi!" He came eyeball to glassy eyeball with Bambi and whimpered, "Poor Bambi!" He was petting the beast's large, inert body when he noticed that Bambi, well, kind of *smelled*. As drunk as he was, Donnie Lee became acutely aware that poor Bambi stunk.

A big arm went around Donnie Lee's frail shoulders, pulling him away from Bambi. "You okay, bud?" It was Avery, leading Donnie Lee away from the poor creature hanging on the wall.

"What happened to Bambi?!" sobbed Donnie Lee.

"Bambi had a little accident. Come on over here and just don't look at it."

"He came to such a sad end!"

"Yeah," sighed Avery, "it's a shame, ain't it?"

"How did it happen?"

Avery didn't have the heart to tell poor, drunk Donnie Lee that Bambi was shot by his cousin Bobby up near Folsom, so he just said, "Car hit him. We couldn't just leave him there, dead in the road."

Donnie Lee shook his head. "Oh no, that would be so cruel! Are you giving him a decent burial?"

Avery knew that by tomorrow night Bambi would morph into an enormous pot of venison stew, among other things, which Donnie Lee in all likelihood would help eat, but now was not the time to mention it. "Sure," said Avery, "me and Bobby, we're gonna put him in the ground, say some prayers over him."

Donnie Lee wiped his eyes on his sleeve. "You're a good man, Avery," he slurred.

"Lemme walk you home, son; I think you need to sleep this off."

Once safely inside his house, Donnie Lee collapsed in a heap on his couch and had a strange dream about chasing Bambi through the swamp while being pursued by wild Indians riding pigs. He awoke a few hours later with a terrific hangover and no memory of the night before. He did wonder where the little rope bracelets came from, but didn't dwell on it. He took a Valium and four aspirin and went back to sleep.

*****

Lucille Fontenot was sitting on her front porch in her pink chenille bathrobe, drinking a Barq's rootbeer, when she saw Donnie Lee park his little sports car on his front lawn and stagger across the street. He was crying about Bambi and petting that goddamn dead deer hanging on the side of Avery's garage. They had a live pig over there, too, but it was tied up and seemed to be drugged because it was just standing there swaying back and forth, not making any noise. Lucille looked over at Telemachus scratching his claws on the porch column and said, "Boy, you better be glad they don't eat cats; they'd have your furry little ass over there, too — they've got every other kind of wildlife." Telemachus gave her a dirty look, then jumped up on the porch swing and began to wash himself.

Lucille watched Avery comfort Donnie Lee and help him back across the street to his house. When Donnie Lee was safely behind his closed front door, Lucille called out to Avery and motioned him over to the porch. Avery ambled over and sat down on the steps next to her.

"What are you doin' up so late, Miss Lucille? We wake you up?"

Lucille shook her head. "I don't sleep much anymore. I finally nod off about four every morning and sleep 'til ten. Just old age."

Avery nodded and leaned back against the column. "It's a pisser, ain't it? Gettin' older. My mama's got arthritis, bursitis, every other kinda 'itis' you can name, includin' ornery-itis."

Lucille grinned and took another swig of her Barq's. "Donnie Lee okay?"

"Yeah, he's just dead drunk. I hope he ain't too sick to make the wedding. I'm kinda looking forward to seeing what kind of costume he shows up in. I just hope he comes as a man this time. Remember when he came to my sister Millie's second wedding dressed up like Marilyn Monroe?" Lucille nodded. "I mean, nobody really cared, but we didn't know quite what to call him." Avery laughed. "And then he set his wig on fire with a cigarette, and my cousin Luther ripped it off his head and threw it in the punchbowl. He's just a walking disaster."

Lucille sighed deeply. "That boy has never been right since he was little. When he was about five or six he used to dress up in his Little Bo Peep costume for Halloween and walk that little dog of theirs around the neighborhood, telling everybody it was his sheep. His mama tried to discourage it for a while, but Donnie was determined to dress up like a girl and act like Tinkerbell. I remember when he was about ten and he dressed up for Mardi Gras as a bride. Some bigger boys beat him up and stole his tiara and veil. Poor little thing, he came dragging back here with a bloody nose and a torn dress and one of his high heels missing. His mama had hit one of the boys with her can of Dixie beer, but she couldn't run fast enough to catch them. They came over here and I gave her a shot of Jack Daniels and little Donnie a Dr. Pepper. That boy used to love Dr. Pepper, drank it all the time, finally gave him a kidney stone when he was in college. The doctor told him if he didn't stop drinking Dr. Pepper he was going to lose a kidney, so he switched to vodka."

Avery yawned and stretched. "I guess he traded his liver for a kidney."

"He didn't drink all that much really until his mama died. Poor baby, he came home one night and found her dead in the bed."

Avery couldn't help but grin. "I remember when it happened. Death by gerbil."

Lucille let out a little laugh. "I know it isn't funny, but it was so bizarre. And poor Donnie was just devastated, blamed himself, sat out there at St. Roc by her vault every day, drinking and crying. Leola found him over there when she was putting flowers on her daddy's vault on All Saints Day, brought him home and put him to bed. He was sick as a dog, had a fever, he was shivering. She said he smelled like he hadn't bathed in a week, so she stripped him down and put him in the shower. She said he was wearing lacy lavender panties and a silk camisole under his clothes and had his little thing tied up with a purple cord. He didn't fight with her at all, just stood there in the shower and cried. She made him an appointment with a psychiatrist and went with him, just to make sure he showed up. He's still in therapy. I guess it's helping him, he seems a lot happier now. Still drinking, just not as much." She set down her empty Barq's bottle and wrapped her arms around her knees. "Wonder what makes him be like that, want to dress up as a girl and sleep with boys?"

Avery sighed. "Some folks are just born different, Miss Lucille."

Lucille adjusted her robe and scooted around to get comfortable on the step. "I understand different. I mean, look at Troy, living over there naked with that girl on the north shore. Drives Leola to distraction, but if she thought about it she'd remember that Troy always liked to go around naked, or as close to it as possible. When he was seven she caught him skinny dipping in his little wading pool in the front yard. She smacked his bottom and made him put on his trunks, but a few days later he was out there sunbathing in the nude. She ran him in the house before he cooked his little weenie. She said she wouldn't have minded so much if nobody could see him but he was out in the front yard and people were calling her to tell her he was naked as a jaybird."

Avery laughed and said, "Remember the time he got arrested for playing golf in the nude?"

"Oh my lord, yes! Well, that was alcohol. He was sixteen and caddying over at Audubon. He and his little caddy friends got drunk one night and thought they'd play a round of strip golf. Troy was the worst golfer in the bunch, so he lost all his clothes first.

Nobody would've even known if they hadn't made so much noise and run the golf cart into the lagoon. Somebody on Walnut Street called and reported a bunch of naked people on the golf course. They all got fired. Leola was just mortified. She blamed it all on Troy's father, but she blames everything on Troy's father, God rest his poor old drunk soul. She's been blaming him for everything since he hung himself on that hooker's brassiere and drowned in the river."

Avery said, "I saw Troy not long ago out at Global Wildlife. He seemed really happy."

"Oh he is really happy; his mama just won't leave him alone 'til he leaves Valerie and puts his clothes back on."

Avery grinned. "He was fully dressed when I saw him. And he's not leaving Valerie any time soon, she's pregnant."

Lucille's mouth dropped open. "You're joking!"

"I am not. She's due in September."

Lucille let all the air out of her body. "Jesus God in heaven. I wonder if they're getting married."

"Oh they're already married, they're been married for the last six months, they just didn't know how to tell his mama."

"Don't you think *now* might be a good time?!"

Avery threw up his hands. "That's up to Troy. He's afraid of her reaction, that's why he hasn't told her about it yet."

Lucille fanned the air. "She won't make much of a fuss. She'll just be so glad he's married. And she'll be thrilled she's about to be a grandma. Troy's her only hope, you know, because Marjory sure isn't going to ever give her any grandchildren."

Avery shook his head. "Not unless she's artificially inseminated. Most lesbians just don't have children. A lot of them adopt, though."

Lucille sighed again. "You really think she's a lesbian?"

"When I was in Atlanta three months ago, I had dinner with Marjory and her girlfriend Jennifer Something-or-Other. I don't remember her last name, she's a stockbroker. They've been living together for the past five years. She asked me not to tell her mother, though, said she would never accept it."

Lucille leaned back and grunted. "Children always underestimate their parents. Leola would still love Marjory if she shaved her head and joined the Hari Krishnas. Of course, she'd rather her be gay than join the Hari Krishnas — she thinks they're all a bunch of wackos." She stood up and grabbed her empty bottle. "Well, I can't tell those kids what to do, but I hope they come to their senses and open up to their mother. She's my best friend; I don't want to see her get hurt by her own children. I won't tell her anything, though; I don't want to get in the middle of it, either. I'm going to bed. Come on, Telemachus, I don't think you're safe out here alone."

Avery chuckled and crossed the street, where the activity was finally dying down. His cousin Eddie was passed out on the ground with his arm thrown over the pig, who was grunting and passing gas in her drug-induced slumber. Avery ducked into his lodge, stepped over various immobile cousins, stripped off his clothes and collapsed into the hammock, where he was soon snoring loud enough to be heard two blocks away.

*****

Miss Libby slipped out her side door and scooted down the alleyway, garden shears in hand. She eased open the fence door and looked down the street to Avery's house. The cousins were making enough noise to cover her movements, and all the action was concentrated at that end of the block — nobody would notice her leaving. She hurried down the sidewalk in the opposite direction, occasionally ducking behind a tree or bush when she got paranoid. Her destination was an oleander bush in the next block, but along the way she pruned a banana tree hanging too far over the sidewalk, a crepe myrtle that caught her hair as she passed underneath its low branches, and a rose bush that plucked at her dress as she brushed past it. Little bits and pieces of foliage littered the dark sidewalk behind her, like the botanical victims of a windstorm.

A low, growling noise, like a boat motor in full throttle brought her up short. She whirled around, searching for the culprit in the hazy streetlight. Suddenly there was a loud snort, like the motor had been snagged in a bush and choked, followed by a long whirring sound. As she stood there in the dark, listening to the cacophony of revving, grinding, snorting and whistling sounds, it began to sound familiar, and suddenly she realized what it was — snoring! She grinned. It was Avery Billiot snoring. She'd heard it for years, especially in the spring and fall when everyone had their windows wide open at night. She just never realized it could be heard from over a block away. That resolved, she turned and continued her way down the street.

Miss Libby understood the consequences if she was ever caught with garden tools again, but she just couldn't help herself, that oleander bush was actually blocking the sidewalk and she was merely doing her civic duty by pruning it. She was cheerfully snipping away at said bush when she heard someone coming down the sidewalk on the other side of the foliage. Specifically, she heard someone drunkenly singing and it sounded like he was headed her way. She quickly hid in the depths of the oleander bush and held her breath, waiting for him to pass.

Leviticus Martin was out for an evening stroll; due to the bottle of Thunderbird he had consumed in the last hour, however, he was a little unsteady on his feet. Leviticus was seventy-two years old and lived in the bottom floor of his sister Corinthian's house. (Leviticus was from a family of twelve brothers and sisters, all named after books of the Bible.) Corinthian was the pastor of the First Church of Heavenly Love and was staunchly opposed to drinking, drugs, gambling, vulgar language and loose women. Since Leviticus was guilty of indulging in four out of five of those deadly sins (he had never indulged in drugs, preferring instead to drown himself in Annie Greensprings, Thunderbird or MD 20/20), Corinthian would not allow him beyond the first floor of her house, but she loved her wayward brother and allowed him to live in the basement. She prayed for him every day and told him he could live upstairs anytime he was ready to see the light and come to Jesus. Leviticus preferred to live in the basement, where he had a kitchen, a bathroom, a comfortable bed and the freedom to drink himself to death.

Leviticus had lost an eye in Korea and part of his mind behind the Birmingham jail ten years later during the Civil Rights movement, when he and his brother Genesis had been beaten and raped by white sheriff's deputies behind the jail, then thrown into a dumpster naked in February. Luckily for the two brothers, this heinous act was witnessed by a white priest who had cut through the alley, heard the commotion and had the good sense to hide behind another dumpster, lest the same fate befall him. He did however, just happen to have a camera in his coat pocket and, thinking this was a golden opportunity to further the cause of justice, snapped photos from his post behind the dumpster. Father Gerald O'Malley was originally an activist from Northern Ireland and no stranger to violence and the fight for civil rights. In fact, a year earlier he had requested a transfer from Boston to Birmingham to be closer to the heart of the "War for Racial Sanity" as he described it. Not that Boston didn't have its own share of racial insanity at the time.

As soon as the deputies had left, Father O'Malley rescued the hapless brothers, wrapped them in plastic sheeting retrieved from the dumpster, and hustled them down the alley and into the back of his panel truck parked two blocks away. He took them to his church, cleaned them up, dressed their wounds, gave them clean clothing, vegetable soup and hot tea, and put them up for the night. The next morning before dawn he hid them in the back of his panel truck and drove them to New Orleans to their brother Deuteronomy's house. Word of the events in Birmingham spread through the neighborhood like wildfire and the large, close-knit family crowded into the little shotgun house until it was bursting at the seams and oozing family members from every orifice. The women cooked and cried, kissed and hugged Leviticus and Genesis so hard it made their ears ring; their Auntee Naomi smothered them in her huge cleavage until they could not take a deep breath. The men stood around in little knots, cursing softly and banging their fists in frustrated rage, making vague threats they knew they could never carry out. Levitucus' father sat in the glider on the porch and cursed until he coughed himself into a fit, then he cried for what he could not do to rectify the situation. Father O'Malley sat beside him and hung his head, feeling utterly ashamed of his race, but he never said a word about the explosive evidence in his coat pocket. The women fed him red beans and gumbo and fried chicken until he could barely walk; the men took up a collection for him, which he tried to refuse, but they pressed the money on him until he graciously accepted. They all thanked him profusely for rescuing their precious family members and pledged their friendship to him for life. And they meant it — Christmas every year brought enough baked goods for him to distribute holiday cheer to the kids at St. Sophia Children's Home; every Easter brought an enormous cardboard box of candy and other goodies, which he handed out to all the kids in his poverty-stricken neighborhood; and the postman delivered a sack full of cards and gifts every birthday. And, come hell or high water, Father O'Malley spent every Mardi Gras with Leviticus' family, one of few white men in a sea of black faces on the sidewalk at the lower end of St. Charles Avenue, clambering for Zulu coconuts on Mardi Gras morning.

Two days after delivering Leviticus and Genesis back to their family, Father O'Malley took a plane to New York and visited with his friend Riley, a journalist with the New York *Times*. A couple of days later, four damaging photos appeared on the front page of the *Times*, with an accompanying story on the Civil Rights movement and the incidents in Birmingham. The black faces in the photos were deliberately fuzzy, but the faces of the white deputies were crystal clear. Father

O'Malley was named as an "anonymous source" only. The story was picked up and run in newspapers across the country. The week after the story appeared, a fifty-five pound box of baked goods was delivered to Father O'Malley with an enormous thank you note signed by one hundred and sixty-seven of Leviticus' family members and friends. They never forgot the Father; he was their hero. When he was killed at a peace rally in Washington, D.C. in 1971, Father O'Malley's primarily white congregation were absolutely amazed when one hundred and five black people from New Orleans showed up at his funeral.

After the incident in Birmingham, Genesis moved to Chicago to work in his uncle's automotive repair shop; he'd had enough of the south and never moved back. Leviticus, on the other hand, never left southeast Louisiana again — in fact, he rarely left Orleans Parish again, preferring the safety and familiarity of his own neighborhood. He worked at various jobs, stayed fairly sober, went to church a lot, got married. But after Father O'Malley's funeral he started to drink in earnest, lost jobs, lost his wife and little boy. He tried AA many times, would stay sober for months, then something would trigger his memories and he would return to the bottle. The pain ran too deep and Leviticus knew of no other way to relieve it.

On this night, as Miss Libby stood hiding in the oleander bush, Leviticus was interested only in relieving his bladder. He stood in front of the oleander bush, aiming low at first but gradually raising his aim higher and peeing all over Miss Libby, who squealed and said, "What do you think you're doing?!"

The disembodied voice literally scared the devil out of Leviticus, who stopped mid-stream and stuttered, "Wh-who's in dere?"

Miss Libby knew it was Leviticus Martin standing on the sidewalk and decided to scare the bejesus out of him, just for fun — and for disturbing her nocturnal passion and peeing on her. "I am the Angel of the Lord," proclaimed Miss Libby, "and I am here to tell you if you drink one more drop of alcohol I will strike you down like a dog!" Then she rustled the bushes ominously. Leviticus screamed hoarsely, threw down his almost empty bottle of Thunderbird, and ran around the corner to his sister's house as fast as his drunken little old legs could carry him. He staggered up the seventeen steps to her porch, banged on the front door and screamed, "Corinthian, lemme in, lemme in!" He continued to bang on the door until Corinthian dragged her two hundred fifty pound frame to the front door. (Like many New Orleanians, Corinthian did not consider overeating a sin but a casualty of living in that fine city where people live to eat, not the other way around.) When Corinthian opened the door she found Leviticus on his knees, one hand pressed to his chest. "I done seen da light," he proclaimed. "Da lawd tole me he would strike me down like a dawg if I ever touched another drop of alkihol! I is ready to come to Jesus!" There was much wailing and "praise da lawd" from Corinthian, whose husband Joshua eventually heard her caterwalling and came to the door to find Corinthian down on her knees alternately crying and praying and her brother passed out on the porch. He carried Leviticus to the bathroom and placed him on the floor because he knew Leviticus would eventually throw up, then dragged his wife back to bed. He surely was glad that it was Leviticus who had passed out and not Corinthian, because he would have had to just leave her fat ass where it lay.

Back at the oleander bush, Miss Libby cursed and picked up her gardening shears. She could not believe she had been pissed on in the line of duty! Maybe it was a sign from God to cut this crap out once and for all. As she dragged her wet, dirty, stinking self back to her house, Miss Libby decided it was finally time to hang up her gardening tools forever.

*****

Leola Broussard put down the quilt she was stitching, pulled off her reading glasses and rubbed her eyes. "Enough of this," she muttered to no one in particular, since no one was there. "I can't see this late at night anyway. Good lord!" She stared at the clock in amazement. Two-thirty. "I had no idea it was this late, no wonder I'm hungry! Think I'll go in the kitchen and eat the rest of that tuna po'boy." She padded into the kitchen, almost tiptoeing in her bare feet. Leola had tiny, pretty feet, like a Japanese Geisha, and she always kept her toenails brightly painted; in contrast, the fingernails on her tiny, childlike hands were always cut short and painted with a clear polish. She used her hands for crafts and gardening too much to keep the nails long or brightly painted.

Leola was tiny all over and had to stretch on the tips of her toes to reach five feet. She only half joked that most ten-year-olds towered over her. Her friend Lucille was only a couple of inches taller, but she was a good twenty pounds heavier and five years older than Leola. And unfortunately, unlike Leola, Lucille looked her age.

Leola opened up the refrigerator door and peered inside. "Now if you eat that tuna, Leola," she mused, "you're gonna be sorry. It'll give you heartburn. Better eat some ham and cheese instead." She sang to herself as she made her sandwich, an old Elvis tune. Leola loved Elvis; she thought he was the best-looking thing on two legs that ever lived. She set the plate on the table, grabbed a coke from the refrigerator, and settled down to eat her sandwich. "Oh, God that's good." She caught sight of her reflection in the mirror over the fireplace. "You look a fright!" she said to the image. "And you've got to stop talking to yourself before they put you in DePaul's! I got to get me another full-time cat. At least it'll give me an excuse to yammer at something all the time. Nobody thinks you're crazy if you talk to your cat." She fiddled with her hair a little, but it was no use, what a mess! "And you're getting older by the minute!" she said to the reflection.

In truth, Leola did not look old at all, she looked like she was in her late 40's. Save a few crow's feet, she had an unlined face, dyed her hair a flattering shade of blonde, and kept her body trim. She was a pretty woman with an oval face and big blue eyes, shapely legs and a trim but curvaceous figure. And although she rarely noticed, she still turned a lot of heads. But her most attractive asset was a sharp wit coupled with an infectious laugh. People were drawn to Leola because she was fun.

After the demise of her second husband, Leola had been courted by quite a few suitors, but most didn't keep her attention for more than a couple of dates. When she first hit the dating trail again, Leola hadn't dated in several years but, as she told Lucille one evening over a plate of double-fudge chocolate brownies and a pitcher of White Russians, she didn't want to spend the rest of her life making love to her sex toys. Lucille said men were more fun to watch on TV than to actually have to eat dinner with or God forbid, live with, but she didn't mind a trip to Bourbon Street every once in a while to have a look at the male strippers. Leola said she wanted more in life than "All My Children" and Bourbon Street strippers.

Leola's first foray into the "dating" world consisted of attending something called a "singles dance", which turned out to be the saddest thing she'd seen since her high school prom, which had been attended entirely by girls and the nuns at St. Mary Elizabeth's. She'd seen more action at her second husband's wake than she saw at the singles dance. She next tried the singles group at church, which held suppers every other Thursday night. Another bomb. The one time she attended she noticed that most of the singles were street people there for the free meal and a few poor souls so old and infirm they must have been brought in from a nursing home — two were using walkers and one old guy was dragging his oxygen tank on a wheelie. Leola ate her red beans and green jello as fast as humanly possibly and ran for her car. A couple of friends set her up with blind dates and she met a few men on her own here and there, but none of it culminated in an orgasmic experience, or even one fun evening. Leola was looking for Mel Gibson in a Ben Stein world. Just about the time she'd decided to give up and call an escort service, her friend Renee Devereaux suggested the personals in the back of *Gambit*.

With a great deal of trepidation, Leola placed an ad in the personals and began to answer a few ads herself. While she was afraid of meeting serial killers, most of the men she met were either lonely, like herself, with few other options, married slimeballs trolling the ads for new nookie, or complete social retards. She discovered why so many men had to date through the personal columns: a lot of men were either cheap or nuts or both. A couple of dates had asked her to split the bill for dinner, and one had gone to the bathroom before the check came and never returned to the table. She had actually gone to the men's room looking for the son-of-a-bitch, but the waiter told her that Mr. Saturday Night had run out through the kitchen door. A man named Larry had taken her to the French Quarter flea market and then picked up a woman in a tight red minidress while Leola was browsing the brass booth. One minute he was behind her looking at a hooka and the next minute she saw him walking into the bar across the street with Ms. Minidress. Leola just sighed, said "good riddance to bad trash," and took the streetcar home.

And then there were the real slimeballs. A guy named Tim had seemed so nice and normal, had an ex-wife and some kids, a good job. But when he got drunk later in the evening and told her he really preferred men, she decided the date was over and asked to be taken home. He behaved like a gentleman and took her home, walked her to her door. But then the little bastard had the nerve to try to kiss her goodnight! She put her hand over his mouth and said, "No, no, honey, I don't where your mouth has been," and closed the door in this face. One blind date told her on the phone that he was more handsome than Rock Hudson, but the man who picked her up that evening looked more like Gene Wilder than Rock Hudson. It was not his misrepresentation of his looks, however, that bothered her, but rather his deplorable table manners. During dinner he quickly became intoxicated and ate like a pig, polishing off not only his own meal in about twenty minutes but also the remainder of her rather large salad. As if that wasn't bad enough, he tipped the salad bowl to his lips and drank the rest of the salad dressing! At that point Leola decided it was time to make a quick getaway through the back door and was excusing herself to make a run for the restroom when Mr. Personality managed to spill a glass of wine all over her silk dress. While she was in the restroom, cursing and trying to wash out the wine, she realized she'd left her purse under the table, therefore making a five yard dash through the kitchen door impossible. She returned to the table to find the Devil Date on his cell phone making a date with another woman. That was when Leola decided to walk home.

After a string of cheapskates, boors, snores, a loser named Sonny who, after two dates, tried to move himself and his seven dogs into her house, and a good looking, exciting man named Charles who said he was a salesman but turned out to be a car thief, Leola declared one Sunday afternoon in Lucille's back yard that she was giving up men forever. Five days later, on a Friday night, she attended her niece Magdalena's wedding and fell madly in love with the groom's father, Luis, over a plate of shrimp etouffee. When she remembered, after her third glass of champagne, that she'd sworn off men forever, Leola thought, well, just one more. It turned out to be a good decision.

Luis Alverado was a ruggedly handsome man and, at sixty-four, still sexy enough to catch the eyes of much younger women. He was just barely five foot seven, but he had the barrel chest, thick shoulders and rippling muscles of a man who had done physical labor most of his life. He owned a plant nursery on the north shore, as well as orchards and a small vineyard, which was now run by his son Ricardo, Magdalena's new husband.

When Luis saw Leola in her pretty pink dress in the buffet line, his heart flipped over twice. He thought she was the prettiest little thing he'd ever seen in his life; she looked just like a china doll. He searched her left hand for a wedding band, saw none, looked at the ceiling and made the sign of the cross, then walked over to the buffet table. He waited until Leola had her plate of food and was looking for a place to sit before he approached her. Luis was a man of direct action. He walked right up to her and said, "You are the most beautiful woman I have even seen." To his surprise, Leola laughed and said, "And you're the best looking thing I've seen since Elvis." Leola found a table, set down her plate of shrimp etouffee and glass of champagne, and stuck out her hand. "I'm Leola Broussard." Luis kissed her hand and said, "I am Luis Alverado, the father of the groom." By the time Leola remembered she'd sworn off men forever, she'd already fallen in love with Luis. They had been together ever since. Last Saturday night, during a romantic dinner at Brigtsen's, Luis had presented Leola with a beautiful four-carat emerald ring and asked her to marry him. She had told him yes, and she had every intention of marrying Luis, but she just wasn't in any kind of hurry. Leola wanted to get married in Lake Tahoe in the early fall. Luis told her anywhere she wanted to go, he would take her there — Hawaii, Mexico, Italy, anywhere. She said no, none of those places, she just wanted to go to Lake Tahoe because she had never been there but had always wanted to see it and now seemed like a good time.

Neither of Leola's other two weddings had been romantic, and her honeymoons had been dismal. Her first husband's idea of a romantic weekend was to go camping and fishing and drink beer at Honey Island Swamp. Leola made him compromise on a weekend trip to Pensacola. Her second husband, who was her first husband's brother, was sweet and dependable but dull. They took a riverboat cruise to Memphis and back, which he thought was the most exciting thing he had ever done, and it probably was. Leola thought it was dreadful; she spent most of the cruise alternately guzzling Dramamine and throwing up over the side of the boat. Her new husband spent most of his time gambling in the saloon. He imagined he was Maverick; Leola imagined herself at home in her own bed and off that goddamned boat. So for her third, and she was certain her last wedding, Leola wanted romance. But she was in no hurry. She had been living alone for a while now and wasn't anxious to share her house. For that matter, she and Luis had not discussed where they were going to live, but Leola didn't want to leave her home; she'd been in her house too long to give it up. She looked at herself one last time in the mirror over the mantle and said, "Well that's settled," and padded off to bed.

*****

Danny Billiot woke up because he was wet. At first he thought he'd just pissed on himself in the night, but even he couldn't have pissed enough to create a pond at the lower end of the back yard by the bamboo hedge. He watched a pink plastic flamingo float by and come to rest on top of his brother Eddie's head. Eddie was resting peacefully next to the soon-to-be roasted pig, who was snoring next to him in a drugged-induced sleep. Danny sloshed over to Eddie and kicked him in the leg. "Hey, bro', wake up before you drown, man!" Eddied shot up out of the water, sputtering and punching the plastic flamingo. He had the flamingo in a headlock before he realized his brother, not the innocent flamingo, had kicked him in his sleep. He hit his brother over the head with the mangled plastic waterbird and said, "What the fuck you doin'?"

Right about that time their Uncle Felix waded over, threw a burlap sack over the pig's head and slashed its throat so fast the befuddled brothers just stood there blinking. Their Cousin Leander, Uncle Felix' son, loaded the pig onto a makeshift stretcher and dragged it over to the other end of the yard to prepare it for barbecue. Danny stood staring at the pig on the stretcher and muttered, "That's cold, man." About that time their cousins Darryl and Judo Dardard bumped into Eddie; they were lugging the deceased Bambi to the same end of the yard as the pig.

Danny pinched his nose and let out a heartfelt, "Pee-ew! I thought *you* smelled bad, bro'!" Eddie hit him again with the flamingo. The boys were slamming each other with faux wildlife when Avery broke up the reverie and demanded to know where all the damned water was coming from. "I dunno, cuz," said Danny. "I woke up in this here river. Damn near drownded!" The brothers abandoned their toys and joined Avery to look for the river's source, which turned out to be the Fellows' house behind them. They discovered the house bleeding water from every crack, running down the steps, into the yard and onto Avery's mother's property and wedding guests. Avery ran up the steps to the side door and pulled it open. A torrent of water washed over the three of them on the steps.

"Fuck me!" yelled Danny as they rushed into the flooded house, scattering in different directions to turn off faucets and open plugged up drains. No one seemed to be home. They searched the house to make sure no one was in there hurt or dead, but when they found Marsha's note scrawled in lipstick on the mirror, they realized why all the faucets had been turned on. They were standing in the living room wondering what to do when Graham Fellows opened the front door.

*****

Graham and Victor had been rehearsing scenarios all the way to Graham's house.

"All we have to do is *look* like we're doing something. We can sit on the couch until Marsha comes downstairs, then go into action," said Graham.

"You gonna just sit there with your drawers down around your knees until the bitch comes downstairs?" giggled Victor.

"Yeah, basically, that's the plan."

Just Off the Streetcar Line

"Can't I just kiss it a little?" whined Victor.

"No you can't kiss it a little!" Graham made a righthand turn onto his street and noticed puddles of water at the curb. "Did it rain last night?" He also noticed that Marsha's car was gone. "Well great, she isn't even here. We'll just have to wait." He parked the car and they got out and climbed the steps to the porch. That was when Graham noticed the water on the porch and saw the Indians inside his house — two of them very wet and muddy — staring at him through the living room window. He opened the front door and squished around on soggy carpet. "What the fuck?"

"Uh, I think your wife tried to drown your house, pal," said Avery. Graham just stood in the middle of the moist room and stared at the Indians. "We came over here because there was a river running through my mother's back yard. The doors were unlocked and there was water everywhere; all the faucets were wide open, man, she meant business!"

Graham finally found his voice and asked, "How do you know it was Marsha who left the faucets running? Maybe it was a burglar."

"Oh sure," said Eddie. "Like maybe it was the wet bandits."

Danny pointed upward. "There's a note on your bathroom mirror, bro', pretty specific."

Graham just nodded. "Oh."

"You wanna see it, man?" asked Danny. "We left it there. Looks like it was written in lipstick."

Graham shook his head. "Naw, I don't care."

"Hey, I'm sorry man," said Avery. "Looks like she left you."

"Big loss," snorted Victor, who noticed the Indians were staring intently at him. "What?"

Eddie shook his head and looked at his cousins. "Nothin', man. It's just, well, I ain't never seen nobody in a suit like that before."

"Do you like it?" preened Victor, adjusting the satin lapels of his lavender jacket. "It's one of my favorites."

Eddie nodded. "Yeah, man, it's cool."

Avery noticed Graham still looked shell-shocked. "Hey, I'm sorry about your wife, man. And your house. Jeez, what a mess!"

"Thanks," said Graham. "I'll get somebody in here to clean up before I sell it. I met a real estate agent over here behind us on the next block; maybe he'd list it."

Avery nodded. "Little Dave, yeah, he'll sell it, he can sell anything."

Graham didn't remember Dave as being especially little, but then Avery was the size of a small grizzly bear. He looked like he bench pressed tree trunks in his spare time. "What about the damage to your mother's property? I'll take care of that, too."

Avery just shook his head. "No damage, except my cousins here got wet."

Eddie nodded. "Yeah, man, but that's 'cause we was passed out on the ground by the pig."

Victor put his soft white hands to his chubby little cheeks. "Pig?"

"Yeah, but don't worry, Uncle Felix slashed its throat already."

Victor made a little chirping sound. These were savages! Wild beasts! And the cleaner one with the long braids had fabulous muscles. Oooh, this was thrilling! Victor just loved big strong manly men.

Avery ignored the little fagot in purple, but he felt a twinge of pity for Graham, although Graham had shown no sorrow over his wife's departure. Not that Avery blamed him — he wouldn't have been sorry to see that screaming meemie bitch hit the road either. "Why don't you come to my wedding tonight? It's in the back yard, around eight o'clock, whenever the medicine person is ready. Right now he's takin' Beano and Imodium AD." He glared at his cousins. "I *told* you not to take him to Boudreau's Burrito House last night! What were you thinkin'? He's an old man; his insides ain't what they used to be."

"But he wanted to go!" protested Eddie. "He heard us talkin' about goin' over there and said he's goin' with us. I told him you told us not to take him cause 'a his delicate insides, and he said 'Avery ain't my mama and I want some 'a them burritos,' so we took him along. I ain't about to tell a medicine man what to eat. Besides, I figured if he could eat nutria at home he could handle Boudreau's."

Avery just looked disgusted. "He's ninety-three years old! Nutria ain't got nothin' on Boudreau's." He sighed and turned back to Graham. "So anyway, ya'll come on over tonight. Any time you want really, the party'll go on all night." He nodded at Victor. "You can bring your, uh, friend."

Graham looked at Victor, who was clapping his hands in delight and bouncing on his toes. Victor loved weddings and funerals; he was already planning his outfit. "Ok, yeah, we'll come," nodded Graham. "Hey, can I bring my girlfriend?"

Avery didn't flick an eyelash. "Sure, man, the more the merrier."

*****

Donnie Lee lay on his big red couch in his Judy Jetson living room and tried valiantly to open one eyelid, but it was too heavy, the effort was beyond his muscular ability just right then. He could hear someone singing somewhere far away and he thought he might be dead. He dimly remembered that someone had killed Bambi, but he couldn't remember why or if it was connected to his current state of paralysis. He listened for another minute, since he was unable to move anyway, and wondered if he was in heaven. Did angels sing Bessie Smith tunes? He wasn't sure about their choice of music, but he pretty sure angels didn't cook bacon and he definitely smelled bacon frying. Maybe he was in hell and the devil was barbecuing his toes! With a great deal of effort, Donnie wiggled his toes; they seemed intact, and he was pretty sure they weren't on fire. He took another experimental sniff. Coffee. No, he wasn't in hell. God had created coffee to keep humans alive and ambulatory day after day; Donnie Lee knew without a doubt that he could not have lived this long without daily assistance from the Caffeine Fairy. At this moment, what he needed was a coffee IV, dark roast.

The singing had stopped and Donnie felt a presence in the room. He gathered all his strength and very slowly opened one eyelid. He saw a big black shape leaning over him. The devil! He *was* in hell! He tried to scream but all that came out was a weak croaking sound, like a dying frog.

"Least you ain't dead," muttered the apparition. "I thought you might be dead when I come in here, but you was snoring, so I knowed right away you was still alive, just dead drunk. Pew-whee, boy, you stink! What is that unnatchul odor?"

By now Donnie Lee had managed to open the other eye to a slit. Why was Miss Beulah standing over him with a glass of blood? He hoped to God it wasn't *his* blood. He knew Miss Beulah practiced voodoo, but he was vague on the details of the religion. Sacrifice! He was scared shitless but too catatonic to move or speak coherently. "Bambi!" he screamed hoarsely.

"Don't know nothin' about no Bambi. Boy, it musta' been some night you had. You know yo' car's parked on toppa' yo' mama's rosebushes? You lef' da top down all night — foun' Tigger sleepin' in it dis mornin'. If somebody'd stole it wif Tigger in dere, Eugenia wouldda been some kinda upset! He liked a' choked hisself to def tryin' to get outta dere — got his collar all hung up on da gear shif'. He was howlin' and shakin', you know how scarified he be. I got him a' loose, but he was so skert, I hadda pick him up and carry him crost da road, and he ain't nothin' light neither. Eugenia hadda give him a couple a' biscuits wif syrup to calm him down. He be awright."

Just when Donnie Lee thought his head might fall off onto the floor, Miss Beulah cut her recitation short and said, "You lookin' kinda green 'round da gills, boy. He'ah, drank dis, fix you up good." Miss Beulah advanced on poor Donnie with the glass of blood, held his nose and poured it down his throat before he could croak at her again. He sputtered and coughed and his eyes watered, but he got down the evil

Just Off the Streetcar Line

mixture and suddenly found his tongue. "Awwwwk! Blood, I drank blood!"

Miss Beulah looked at him with disgust. "What's got into you, boy? Didn't give you no blood to drank. Is you seein' stuff again? Boy, dat demon alkihol, it makes peoples plumb crazy! Dat be tomato juice I give you wif a egg, some tobasco an' coffee grounds and jes' a tech a' frog tongue. You gonna live."

Donna Lee noticed he suddenly felt a little less like he was in the throes of death; in fact, he was feeling much better — the room had stopped spinning, his stomach had stopped doing back flips, and his head had settled down to a dull ache. As his head cleared and he started to regain his motor functions, Donnie started to wonder why Miss Beulah was in his house cooking bacon. "How come you're cooking in my house?"

"Da UPS man tried to deliver a package yestidy, but you wasn't answerin' da do', so I signed for it. It be from da Fantasy Fairy and it be biiiiiiig. You order one a dem blowed up dolls like po' little Ant'ny crost da' street? He's drivin' his po' mama plum loco. She 'bout to dispair a' him ever bein' normal."

Donnie pulled himself up off the couch and picked up the big box in the middle of the floor. "It's not a doll, Miss Beulah, it's my costume for the Fairies and Friends Ball Tuesday night. It came! I was afraid it wouldn't get here in time."

"Well, honey, you go gets yo'self cleaned up. You be ripe! I don' know what you been rollin' in, but you need to burn dem cloz. Soon's you get a baf you can come eat yo' breakfast I made. You don't eat nothin', you down to skin n' bones, you look like a skeleton 'fore long, you keep drankin' and not eatin'. Now go on! I'll set the table."

Donnie Lee grabbed his box and shuffled off toward the bathroom. Half an hour later he reappeared, squeaky clean, slathered with gardenia lotion, and attired in a shiny purple body suit, flowery headpiece and big glittery lavender fairy wings. "It fits!" he announced.

Miss Beulah thought he looked like a deranged purple Big Bird, but she kept her opinion to herself. She didn't want to hurt poor little Donnie's feelings — he was delicate. "You look real nice, baby. An' you smell better, too. Now eat yo' breakfas'." She sat down at the table with him and poured both of them a cup of coffee. She didn't really want any coffee, but she wanted to make sure Donnie Lee ate. He looked like a little refugee as it was, and that skin-tight purple costume didn't help any — it made him look like an insect. Ever since Donnie had lost his mama in that tragic accident, he'd been going straight to hell. Miss Beulah wanted to talk to Donnie and help him, but now was not a good time. She didn't think she could keep a straight face telling a grown man wearing fairy wings why he shouldn't drink. So she rambled on about her family while Donnie ate, then she cleared away the dishes and put them in the dishwasher.

Donnie Lee was preening in the hall mirror when the doorbell rang. He opened the front door to see two startled looking black women looking back at him. They were holding bibles and fanning themselves with tracts that read, "Is Jesus driving your car?" They both looked back at Donnie's car on the lawn, straddling his mother's rose bushes. "Good morning, ladies," he said brightly.

"Uh, good afternoon, uh, sir. We've come to talk to you about the Lord."

Just as Donnie was trying to come up with a way to politely rebuff the Jehovah's Witnesses, they both looked behind him and screamed. "The devil woman!" They turned tail and ran down the stops and roared down the sidewalk before he could even open his mouth. He turned and looked at Miss Beulah standing behind him in the dining room, her arms folded across her ample chest and a grim look on her face. "Dem's crazy women," she announced.

"Yes, ma'am," nodded Donnie Lee.

Miss Beulah made her way to the door and said, "I be goin', now. I gots to get ready for da weddin'. I be seein' you tonight, honey." She kissed one cheek and patted the other, then lumbered off to her own house next door.

"The wedding!" squeaked Donnie Lee. He scurried off to his bedroom to prepare his outfit, lavender fairy wings flapping furiously as he ran.

*****

Jackie Cheramie stood in the middle of her den, looking down at the little piles of cash and coins spread out all over the dark blue rug. Lisa was in her bedroom, sleeping off three Martinis and a Valium. Louie had gone home to change for the wedding, refusing payment for his part in rescuing Lisa, declaring that he was rich enough, having won $750 at a slot machine at the airport. Besides, he'd been lucky enough to meet Miss Nude World in the elevator at the MGM Grande, a true highlight in his life. The fact that she had been wearing a pink jogging suit and carrying a little white teacup poodle at the time did nothing to diminish the experience of sharing an elevator with his fantasy woman — even when her fantasy dog peed on his shoes. Miss Nude World had been extremely apologetic and offered to buy Louie a new pair of Nikes, but he'd declined her offer. After all, how many people could claim to have been peed on by Miss Nude World's dog in a Las Vegas elevator? Jackie didn't know and didn't care, she just wanted out of Fantasy Land as quickly as possible.

Even though Jackie had had visions of having to smuggle Lisa out of Las Vegas one step ahead of the police, their plane lifting off as the frustrated cops watched from the runway, the three intrepid travelers

Just Off the Streetcar Line

weren't given a second look by anyone other than the usual assortment of hookers and con artists milling around the big hotel. Jackie had insisted Lisa wear baggy clothes and a black wig she purchased from a mall, but no one had given the little entourage or Lisa's makeup bag more than a fleeting glance.

Jackie sat down on the carpet and methodically arranged all the cash in a fireproofed metal box, all but three hundred dollars and a handful of quarters, which she locked in a desk drawer. Then she took a screwdriver and removed the mirror from above the mantel and opened the safe behind it. There she added the latest metal box to five other metal boxes, entered the amount in a small notebook, then closed it up and screwed the mirror back in.

Absolutely no other living person knew about the safe behind the mirror. Before she died, Jackie's grandmother had shown the safe and its contents to Jackie, had sworn her to secrecy forever, then made her commit the combination to memory. At the time the safe had held only two fireproof boxes, one filled with gold coins stolen by Jackie's great-great-grandfather from a gambling boat in 1887. The other box contained a rather larger assortment of fine jewelry, most of it stolen by a French jewel thief named Jean-Jacques who had been madly in love with Jackie's great-grandmother. Sadly, Jean-Jacques had been killed at the height of his career by a boa constrictor named Valentino when he'd attempted to escape through the conservatory of a wealthy Italian adventurer he'd just robbed. Jean-Jacques' body was discovered the next day by the snake handler, right about the time the adventurer's wife discovered that most of her jewelry was missing. When a frantic search of the mansion turned up no jewelry, an astute young policeman noticed a peculiar bulge in Valentino's midsection and the mystery was solved. Alas, poor Valentino, he gave up his life for half a million dollars worth of jewels, not a paltry sum in 1923.

The sun was going down and the singing down the street was getting louder. Jackie pulled open the curtains and raised the window. A warm breeze and the sound of drums blew through the window, along with the sweet scent of the olive tree in the front yard. There is nothing in this world like the scent of an olive tree in bloom. It always made Jackie hungry and horny at the same time. She watched two men in uniform block off both ends of the street while four old women set folding chairs in the middle of the road. Neighbors were streaming into the street and Avery's relatives were everywhere, pouring out of cars, the house and yard, piling gifts and food on table tops, cooking, singing, drumming, laughing, yelling at each other. One old man in a calico ribbon shirt was hollering at a young man in braids dragging something along the ground. "Don't brang that carcass over here, it'll stink up the whole block! Wrap it up in this here tarp and stick it in the garage with the pig leavings." Which is what they did. Jackie suspected that by tomorrow afternoon it would take a biohazard team to clean out the garage, but right now she really didn't care. It was time to take a bath and dress for the wedding.

*****

As Avery sat on the toilet contemplating his future, fending off relatives anxious to invade his domain, he decided that a house simply could not have too many bathrooms. He didn't know how the family had survived in this house for so long with three kids and only one bathroom. When they finally left home, Avery and his siblings had all made housing with multiple bathrooms a top priority in their lives. And when Avery came home after his divorce, the first thing he had done was install another bathroom in his mother's house.

Bam, bam, bam! "Avery, you in there?"

"No, Uncle Vernon, I ain't in here, I done flushed myself down the toilet. This is a recording. Leave a message at the sound of the beep."

"I got to go. Them nutria sausage I ate a while ago is tryin' to slide out my ass."

Avery sighed. He was sympathetic, but a heaping plate of red beans and rice plus four cups of coffee were knocking at this back door. "There's another bathroom off the kitchen, go in there."

"Your Aunt Tippy's in there. There ain't gonna be no seat left when she leaves. Don't know how that woman wipes her ass. Bet she has to use the hose instead a' the terlet paper." Aunt Tippy was four hundred pounds if she was an ounce. After breaking eight toilet seats in one year, her husband Ollie had finally installed a stainless steel seat, declaring, "Woman, if you breaks *dat* terlet seat, I's staplin' yo' mouf shet and settin' yo' big ass down in a hole in da' back yard!"

"Go away," grumbled Avery. "You're makin' my ass shrink up!"

"Well where'm I supposed to go?"

Avery sighed again. "There's a port-o-potty out back."

"There's a line for that!"

Avery thought for a few seconds, then remembered his neighbor to the rear. "Hey, Unc, go behind us to the Yankee people's house, that blue house right behind us. The doors are unlocked and the guy it belongs to said we could use it all weekend; he ain't livin' there."

"I ain't goin' over there, there's a crazy woman livin' in that house! Last time we was here, she called us a bunch of filthy savages, and we weren't doin' nothin' but killin' squirrels with my pellet gun in the back of the house. Didn't none a' them squirrels have her name on 'em neither. I even offered her a few of 'em, told her how to skin 'em and cook 'em. That's when she called us filthy savages. She threatened to cut my braid off with her hedge clippers! I said sistah, I bathes every day but I smells yo' ugly white ass from down the block! You smells worse'n my pig Leonard! She started screamin' cuss words at me and Titus and Boudreaux, so we duct taped her to the lawn chair. Last time we saw 'er, she was runnin' down the street all bent over in the chair. Don't know who cut her a' loose."

Avery tried not to laugh because it backed up the gas and hurt, but the thought of the Yankee lady running down the street duct taped to a chair was a side splitter. Avery laughed until he doubled over and gasped in pain. "She don't live there no more, Unc. She up and hit the road, tried to drown the house, left all the water running all over the place. So you can go over there and drop your drawers. Ain't nobody gonna both you."

"Awright. I ain't too particular where I drops 'em at this point."

Yes indeed, thought Avery, wherever me and Samantha live, we're gonna have plenty of bathrooms! Just where they were going to live after their honeymoon was a mystery, but they would figure it out. All of Avery's rental property was rented out, but they could come back to his mother's house and either rent or buy something pretty fast, there was never a dearth of housing in New Orleans. And they were definitely settling down in New Orleans.

Avery had made it very clear that he was not leaving the city of his birth unless all the levees broke or the city sank under the weight of its own corruption, neither of which was out of the realm of possibility. Samantha said she understood and, having been a nomad most of her life, would just as soon settle in New Orleans as anywhere else. She had had something like forty-seven addresses in her forty-three years of life on this planet and she was ready to light somewhere.

Avery could not imagine wandering around from place to place like that. An extended vacation was one thing, but moving around all over the country was quite another. He had never lived outside southeast Louisiana and couldn't imagine living anywhere else. Why in the world would anybody want to live someplace else anyway? Why, this was the center of the Universe! Besides, once you crossed the state line, you could starve to death trying to find a decent meal. Avery knew from experience — he had traveled as far north as Buffalo, New York and as far west as San Francisco, California. He had graciously eaten what was provided, but he always lost weight on those trips out of state. The one exception was New Mexico — he always gained weight when he went to New Mexico. After one two-week trip to Taos, he returned to New Orleans twelve pounds heavier. New Mexico was the only other state he could imagine living in, and he often thought of buying a house out there and living out west in the summer, but it never crossed his mind to leave New Orleans for more than a few months out of the year. He had discussed this plan with Samantha, who had said,

"Let's just do it. Whatever you want is fine with me, so long as we're together." At that moment, Avery knew for certain that he had found the right woman.

*****

Louie grabbed a beer from a big tin tub and wandered among the guests doing what he did best, observing. The vows had been short. An ancient looking Indian who spoke heavily accented English had spoken some words in another language — somebody said it was Choctaw — then he sang a song in some other language that sounded like a strange mix of French and Hebrew. They smoked a pipe, he said some more prayers. After that he asked the couple if they loved each other enough to stay together. They said they did. He asked them if they would be true to each other, and the bride replied, "If he wants to live a long, healthy life he will be." Avery's brother, the best man, handed each of them a piece of leather braid, which they tied around each other's wrists. Then Avery's mother placed a broom with a white bow tied to the handle on the ground, and the bride and groom clasped hands and jumped over the broom (actually, the bride jumped — Avery grunted and stepped over it). With that, the old medicine man said, "You're married. Now go on about your business." There were some war whoops and then some old guy in a purple suit signed a piece of paper. After that the partying began in earnest. A big, hulking Indian wearing a red bandana standing in front of Louie turned to a skinny little guy standing next to him and said, "That's Avery's cousin Leroy Charbonet. He's a

Dardard on his mother's side. He's a judge, so he can sign the license. Grandfather J.J. ain't no priest or nothin'; he can't legally marry people." An Indian in a calico shirt standing next to Red Bandana said, "How'd he get to be a judge?" Red Bandana said, "His relatives voted for him."

People were scattered everywhere, in small groups and large, all over yards, the street, on front porches — the wedding was literally a block party, with cop cars parked at each end of the block. A mixed bag of chairs, stools, lawn furniture, a couple of couches, some beanbag chairs and several picnic table benches were strewn haphazardly over the landscape, and a motorized barca-lounger driven by an elderly Indian with a long white braid whizzed up and down the street. As the night wore on, the guests were entertained by the barca-lounger driver and a very large old woman in a pink mumu riding a senior citizen shopping scooter. The senior avengers drag raced up and down the block, screaming obscenities at each other in French and creating a near riot on the sidelines as a flurry of betting ensued. The old lady won, two out of three. This nouveau sporting event brought out other motorized household and garden implements for a little impromptu drag racing, including a riding lawn mower, a kid's electric scooter, an industrial floor buffer and some type of pink Barbie vehicle driven by a skinny Indian kid in cammo. The old lady in the shopping scooter ran the kid and the Barbie-mobile into the ditch, screaming, "Eat this, Barbie doll!" It was the most entertaining sporting event Louie had ever witnessed. His only regret was that he did not have his camcorder with him at the time.

Louie had never seen so much food in all his born days. During the long evening he tried to sample a little of everything: roast pig, barbecued goat, nutria sausage, venison stew, raw oysters, fried softshell crabs, jars and jars of pickled veggies, jambalaya, shrimp etouffee, corn machoux, fried catfish, chicken gumbo, alligator on a stick, turtle soup, snake sauce picante, cracklins, red beans and rice — there seemed to be no end to the fabulous food. Then there were the sweets: not just the bride's cake, which was pink and topped with an enormous sugar crawfish and studded with black cherries, and the groom's cake (chocolate cake shaped like an alligator and swimming in a pond of raspberries and mint leaves), but also every conceivable type of cake, pie, cookie, candy and other delicacy. There was literally enough food to feed a platoon — and enough booze to keep them all drunk for days. In addition to all the store-bought beer and wine (the groom's mother would not allow hard liquor at the wedding), there were bottles and bottles of homemade wine — if some type of fruit or flower could be fermented in a bottle, it had found its way to the wedding. Louie finally collapsed in a semi-coma in a hammock strung up between two olive trees, unable to consume another morsel of food or another drop of liquid. Since he could do little more than lay in the hammock like an old rag doll and breath in and out, Louie passed the time watching other guests until he fell into a deep slumber.

*****

While Louie lay comatose in the hammock, Anthony Guidry was standing not far from him in a little grove of bamboo, drinking a Turbo Dog beer and hiding from his mother. The news of his moving out had not gone over well. Rosemarie had cried and moaned that he would starve to death on his own, probably turn into an alcoholic like those no-good friends of his. Anthony had responded by locking himself in his bedroom and preparing for the wedding. In order to further avoid confrontation, he had crawled out of his window and was lowering himself to the ground when he looked around and noticed Jackie Cheramie standing on the sidewalk across the street, holding a wedding present and staring at him. While trying to get a better look at her long legs extending from a black and white mini-dress, he lost his balance and landed right smack in a gardenia bush. Jackie just shook her head at him and sashayed across the street with her gift. Now Anthony's pride was wounded and he smelled like a funeral parlour. He could not *wait* to move out of this neighborhood.

Just as Anthony was watching his mother lumber from food tray to food tray, waiting for her to turn her back to him so he could make a break for the street, the most beautiful creature he had ever seen floated by in a cloud of green chiffon and Paloma Picasso perfume. She was accompanied by the Yankee guy from next door and some flamer in a tangerine-colored suit. The more he stared at the beautiful blonde, who looked to Anthony like she might faint, the more she looked familiar. He was absolutely certain he knew her from somewhere, but he couldn't remember her name. As Anthony stood and stared at the blonde goddess, trying to remember anything that would lead his brain to her identity, he heard someone screech, "Victor!" Anthony shrank further into the bamboo as Donnie Lee rushed by in a shiny white suit and top hat and grabbed the tangerine dream by his satin lapels. They hugged, they kissed, they did a little bump dance, then Donnie Lee said, "What in God's name are you doing at Avery's wedding?"

"I'm here with Isabella and her fiancé, Graham. You remember Isabella?"

"Darling! Of course I do!" Donnie hugged and kissed Isabella. Donnie Lee was a little confused. The last time he'd seen Isabella was about three months ago at a big Mardi Gras party in the Hilton ballroom; she'd been liplocked on the dance floor with some little Spanish chick who was wearing the most stunning Balenciaga gown and a diamond and ruby necklace that must've been worth a small fortune. And Graham was the Yankee guy who lived across the street from him with that awful woman who screamed at everyone. Did this mean Marsha had left the neighborhood? He certainly hoped so! That horrid woman had screamed at him twice for parking on her lawn when he'd arrived home just a wee bit tipsy a couple of mornings in a row when he had accidentally mistaken her lawn for his. He would have moved his car, all she had to do was ask.

And she didn't have to dump all her trash inside his precious sports car the second time he'd parked there; he had to get it professionally cleaned after that! He'd sent her a copy of the bill, but she'd ignored him totally and even flipped him the bird and called him a "fucking flamer" when he said hello to her one afternoon! He ignored her after that and kept his car on his side of the street. All these questions were running rampant through his brain, but Donnie Lee politely kept his thoughts to himself and trotted off with Victor to find champagne.

Just as the fog cleared in Anthony's brain and he thought, "That's it!" he heard Miss Leola exclaim, "Isabella Matassa, as I live and breath!" She hugged and kissed Isabella, then introduced her to some Mexican guy Anthony had seen around the neighborhood. "This is my fiancé, Luis." Isabella and Luis shook hands, then Leola turned and yelled, "Lucille, get over here!"

Miss Lucille joined the little group, looked at Isabella and let out a squeak, the hugged her and said, "Where've you been, baby? You still living in the Quarter, honey?"

"Yes, ma'am," said Isabella politely. "Still there."

Miss Leola said, "Isabella Matassa! I haven't seen you since your grandmamma's funeral five years ago!"

"Oh Leola," said Miss Lucille, "it's not Matassa anymore. What was your husband's name, darlin'?"

"Fairchild. But he died years ago, Miss Lucille."

"Yes, darlin', I know and I'm so sorry about that. Your mama told me about it. You were so good to your mama, honey, taking care of her when she was so sick. Everybody loved your mamma."

"I know," said Isabella. "She was the sweetest woman on earth. She never would move out of that house, though, even when she couldn't climb the stairs anymore. I put her in the den downstairs and hired two nurses to move in and take care of her."

"Miss Letty and Miss Betty," said Miss Leola. "The Cuccia sisters. They were awfully good to your mother, and she loved them. It was very sweet of you to buy them a house after your mamma died, honey."

"It was the least I could do," said Isabella. "They took such good care of her."

"What about you, darlin'?" asked Miss Lucille. "Are you happy, honey? Did you ever remarry?"

Isabella smiled and turned to Graham, whom everyone seemed to notice for the first time. Graham looked like a deer caught in the headlights on the highway. Anthony held his breath and waited.

"I'm getting married again," said Isabella. "This is my fiancé, Graham."

No one spoke for five seconds, then Miss Leola smiled at Graham and said, "Well hello again, Mr. Fellows. I heard your wife ran off, sweetie, but I'm so glad you and Isabella have each other. Isabella's a wonderful woman and we love her. You take good care of her, now, you hear?"

"Yes ma'am, I will," said Graham, who was feeling a little sick to his stomach.

Isabella turned to Graham and asked, "How do you know Miss Leola?"

"I bought the house back here," he said, jerking his thumb in the direction of his soon-to-be ex-house.

Isabella stared at him in disbelief. "You bought my mamma's house?! I knew you'd bought a house on this street, I just never realized which one! I sold it ten years ago to a man named Barry Plaissance."

"Oh honey," chimed in Miss Lucille, "they moved to Raceland last year to live with their daughter. She got a job working offshore and somebody had to take care of her little girl while she was gone. She's needed help ever since her no-good husband ran off with that girl who dances naked with a snake. I couldn't do it myself."

Just Off the Streetcar Line

"What?" asked Miss Leola. "Run off with a stripper?"

"Dance with a snake," said Miss Lucille. "I just can't imagine something like that crawling all over my naked body."

Anthony couldn't imagine it either. Just the thought of Miss Lucille doing a hoochie coochie dance with a snake was enough to shrivel up his poor little penis to the size of a cocktail sausage. Just as this unappetizing thought crossed his mind, Miss Leola looked right at him and said, "Anthony, honey, your mamma said to tell you when you crawl back in the window tonight would you please use the ladder in the garage instead of the rose trellis like you did the last time when you got all scratched up and pulled the trellis down with you and Mr. Charlie had to come over and shoot the lock off the door."

Anthony stood frozen in his hiding place and just said, "Yes ma'am."

As the little group dispersed and Miss Leola and Miss Lucille wandered toward one of the buffet tables, he heard Miss Leola say, "That boy just drives his mamma to distraction."

Anthony rustled his way out of the bamboo and hurried toward the sidewalk, thinking, "I got to get outta here quick! It's just too mortifying living in this damned neighborhood."

*****

Rosemarie Guidry watched her son emerge from his hiding place in the bamboo stand. She shook her head and muttered, "That boy will be the death of me yet." She was polishing off her third stuffed merliton when Leola and Lucille pushed their way through the crowd to sample the barbecued oysters piled on a wrought iron table at Rosemarie's elbow. Leola was moaning over the delectable oysters when Lucille suddenly said, "Oh my lord, look at this comin' here!" Leola looked up to see her second-born child bearing down on her, followed by an obviously pregnant Valerie. She was so shocked to see them (and fully dressed) that she dropped her oyster. "Troy!"

Troy gave his mother a hug and a kiss and said, "Hey, mamma."

Leola whacked him over the head with her purse. "Don't you 'hey mamma' me! Where've you been for the last three months, in deepest, darkest Africa?!" She eyed Valerie reproachfully. "Obviously you've been busy. Just when did you plan on telling me I'm going to be a grandmother?"

"I'm telling you now!"

Leola him her recalcitrant son with her purse again. "This is all Vinnie's fault! If he'd been here, you never would've gone off to live nekkid in the woods and have illegitimate babies and make your mother crazy!"

"Who's making illegitimate babies? We're married!"

At this announcement, Leola's mouth dropped open. "What?!" She whacked Troy with her purse again. "You didn't even invite your own mother to the wedding!" Whack! Whack!

Troy grabbed the purse and said, "There wasn't any wedding, we just went to the courthouse in Covington."

Leola finally started to cry. "You didn't even get married in a church! I never got to see my baby boy get married." At this she cried harder. "This is all Vinnie's fault!" Troy put his arm around his mother but could think of no reply that would help. He looked over at Lucille, who had her arms folded across her chest and was glaring at him. No help there. Leola finally slowed the waterworks and sniffled. "Does your sister know about this? Am I the last one to find out?"

Troy looked uncomfortable. "Uh, actually, Marjory knew about it and, uh, well, she's out in the car."

"What do you mean, 'out in the car'?! Whose car?"

"My car. She came with us."

Leola looked completely bewildered. "Why in the world is she sitting in your car?"

Troy stuck his hands in his pockets and cleared his throat a few times. "Well, actually, she's sitting out there with her girlfriend."

Leola gave him a blank look. "You're not making any sense, Troy."

Troy pulled on his collar. "Well, Mamma, she's afraid you won't like her girlfriend."

"Why, is she socially repulsive?"

"No, she's a perfectly nice woman named Jennifer."

Leola was getting exasperated. "Then why the hell wouldn't I like her?"

Troy sighed. "Marjory is afraid you'll hate her if you find out she's a lesbian."

"A lesbian? My daughter is a lesbian? Oh, thank God! I thought she was involved with a married man!"

Troy looked confused. "You're not upset?"

"Of course I'm upset! I'm upset because my children are morons! You run off and get married and don't even tell me about it, and now I find out I'm going to be a grandmother! And your sister is hiding out in the car like a ten-year-old! Go get your sister and her girlfriend." As Troy hurried off to retrieve Marjory and

Just Off the Streetcar Line

Jennifer, Leola looked at Lucille and said, "This is all Vinnie's fault!"

*****

Jackie Cheramie was running very late when she left the house with her gift. She'd witnessed the bizarre drag racing from her window and decided to wait until it was over before she tried to cross the street; she didn't want to get run over by a floor buffer. She was standing on her front lawn when she noticed that weird Anthony Guidry lose his grip on his window sill and fall into the gardenia bush. He was always spying on her from across the street with binoculars, so she often left her blinds open and danced around in her underwear just to torture him. She dropped her gift in Avery's dining room with about a thousand other gifts. As she wandered through the kitchen door, she noticed large bulky objects on the back porch; these were gifts that were too large to be wrapped or fit in the dining room or living room, so Avery's mother had tagged them and written who they were from. There seemed to be a large collection of sporting goods, as well as a bundle of furs, a big roll of leather, a pile of antlers, a weaving machine, a bass boat, and what looked like a car motor. Jackie grabbed a beer from a big metal tub in the back yard and wandered around, getting a kick out of the other guests, listening to snatches of conversation.

"You can't skin a gator with that little bitty knife, you got to use one like this here."

"That ain't no knife, it's a machete!"

"Naw, it ain't no machete, this *here's* a machete."

Both knives looked like sabers to Jackie and she quickly moved along.

"We drained that pig and drained that pig."

"What'd you do with the blood?"

"It's over there in the garage. Hope nobody thinks its paint."

Remind me to stay out of that garage, thought Jackie.

".... lost his grip on the gator. We shot the gator but couldn't find Claude nowhere."

"He ever surface?"

"Yeah, he turned up downstream about three days later with most of his face eaten off by critters. Scared the shit out of Lebeau when he fished him out with his pirogue pole. Said he wouldn't have knowed it was Claude 'cept for those nekkid lady undershorts he give him for Christmas last year. His pants was gone, but he was wearing the nekkid lady drawers."

After this grisly little tale, Jackie decided to mingle with the mixed couples and the women for a while.

"I swear, I've never seen anything like it. That lady was chained to the bed with her mouth taped shut! I thought that shit only happened in movies!"

"You're makin' this up, aren't you, Dave?"

"No, no. I swear on my daddy's grave, it happened! I saw it with my own two eyes. Guy's a sicko, man, one of those S&M freaks."

"Did the cops put him in jail?"

"Hell yeah, they put his ass in jail! She was screamin' her head off, threatening to burn him alive, barbecue his balls."

"You blame her?"

"Hell no, I don't blame her one bit!"

Jackie wondered if she'd read about this little episode in the *Times-Picayune* but doubted it — people tended to keep things like that quiet. She had no idea who they were talking about, and now they'd switched to a story about some guy named Boxcar, so Jackie moved on through the crowd, eavesdropping as she went because she couldn't help but hear all the little snatches of conversation around her.

"Your grandmamma is driving me outta my mind! First she was raving at the medicine man about heathens until he hollered, 'Woman, shut up! I'm trying to eat my alligator burrito!' Then she went over by the drum and was singing with the Indians for a while until they started singing about some woman with three tits and she left."

"Where is she now?"

"She's sitting over by the tipi with some old lady who brought her dog. I don't think she's right, either, talks to the dog like it's human."

"That's just Miz Robichaux with Tigger, she's alright. Come on, let's sneak some champagne while Grandmamma isn't looking."

Jackie moved on to a group of Indian women in braids and mumus, all speaking French. Jackie spoke French, but theirs was so different from what she'd learned in school that she could hardly understand them. It sounded like they were talking about some woman named Tutti who burnt most of her hair off with a curling iron, then rode her motorized chair to the grocery store but it spun out of control in the aisles and pulled down an entire display of cheese doodles. The woman telling the story switched to English suddenly and said, "They was squashed cheese doodles ever'where. Poor Tutti was so dizzy from spinnin' around, when they finally caught her and turned off her chair, she was seein' double and she'd lost her fishin' hat that was coverin' up her head. They called Nathan and he come and git her in da' truck, but she been hidin' in the house ever since." Then they switched back to their funny French and Jackie couldn't make out much, so she headed over toward a group of women all

As they passed by the hammock where Louie lay, out cold and snoring, Jackie leaned over and kissed him on the forehead. "My hero," she muttered. He had slept through the entire incident. Impulsively, Jackie pulled off her black lace panties and stuffed them into Louie's shirt pocket. "There you go, Sir Gallahad, first prize."

Jackie looked up to see Avery grinning at her. "I'll explain later," she said, following him and Lisa to the back door.

"Avery?" asked Jackie.

"Yeah, babe?"

"Where's your bride?"

Avery pointed in the direction of the tipi. "She's over there with my cousin Luther. He expressed some interest in her little thirty-two."

"She's packin' on her wedding day?!"

"Thigh holster," grunted Avery. "When things got cranked up around here last night, she thought it might get a little rowdy tonight, too. She's no fool." He held the back screen door open for Lisa and Jackie, who gave a quick look back at the guests cavorting among the plastic wildlife, and followed them inside.

*****

Just Off the Streetcar Line

Something was tickling Louie's ear. He swatted at it a couple of times, but the tickling didn't stop. He finally opened up his eyes and saw Coceaux's face looming over him. "Scoot over," she said, "I'm climbing in with you." The very surprised Louie scooted over in the hammock to make room for the love of his life.

"What are you doin' here?" he asked.

"Lookin' for you," said Coceaux, giving him a kiss. "Didn't know there'd be a block party goin' on."

"It's a wedding," said Louie.

"This is a wedding?"

"Yep."

"Whose wedding?"

"Avery's wedding. You remember Avery?"

"Big Indian?"

Louie twisted in the hammock to get comfortable. "That's the one."

"Looks like a hell of a party."

"It is. I think I ate about forty pounds of food tonight."

Coceaux smiled at him. "You'll get fat."

wearing red hats and purple suits. Apparently they'd all come straight to the wedding from a Ya-Ya Sisterhood meeting and were going on and on about somebody's sister wetting her pants and how hard it was to stay continent at their age. Jackie grew bored very quickly and moved away from the Depends group.

Just as she turned away from the Ya-Yas, Jackie looked toward her house and saw Lisa crossing the road. Lisa had obviously awakened and remembered the wedding, because she was dressed up in a pretty blue Chinese pajama outfit. As she watched her mother walk into Avery's yard, she noticed how thin she looked; she also noticed a sleazy looking man following Lisa, and he looked none too happy. Frank, the asshole Lisa had shot in Las Vegas. Lisa, of course, was oblivious to the impending trouble fast approaching her. Jackie emptied her beer onto the ground and grabbed the bottle by the neck, then moved toward her mother as quickly as she could in the thick crowd.

Frank got to Lisa first and grabbed her by the hair with one hand and slapped her with the other then threw her to the ground. Lisa screamed just as Jackie, beer bottle in hand, jumped onto Frank's back and hit him over the head with the bottle. He easily threw Jackie off then backhanded Lisa. Jackie jumped up and was raising the beer bottle to hit Frank again when Avery's big brown paw reached out and spun him around; with the other paw he grabbed Frank by the neck and lifted him off the ground. Frank started to wiggle and was trying to punch Avery with his right hand, but his arms were suddenly grabbed by people who looked very much like Indians, then he noticed that he was surrounded by people who were not only Indians but also very hostile, some of them with painted faces and feathers in their hair, and all of them armed. One rough looking guy actually had a machete in his hand, and a young Indian had a crossbow pointed at Frank's head. There were also at least five or six guns pointed at Frank. "Now," rumbled Avery, "the way I see it, pal, you got three choices: one, you can struggle and take a swing at me and cause more trouble over here and we kill you on the spot; two, you calm down but keep being an asshole and my cousin Joey here takes you to jail; or three, you apologize to this lady and go away quietly and never bother her or come near her again and we'll let you go. If you give us any argument, you're going to either jail or the morgue. You understand?"

Frank, upon seeing his options were severely limited, nodded and Avery put him down. The slimeball apologized to Lisa, who was crying and hiding behind Joey, then quickly made his exit from the party and ran off toward Magazine Street. Jackie was certain he would never bother Lisa again, but she was also certain that as long as Lisa lived, there would always be another Frank somewhere down the road. Avery and Jackie took Lisa to the house so Avery could tend to Lisa's bruises.

Avery looked over at Jackie and said, "I guess no one will ever forget *this* wedding, huh?"

Jackie shook her head. "Not likely."

Just Off the Streetcar Line

"Probably. Will you love me anyway?" asked Louie.

"Probably," said Coceaux. She pulled a pair of black panties out of Louie's shirt pocket and dangled them in his face. "Yours?"

Louie examined the panties, then grinned. "I'm not sure, but I think this is payment for services rendered."

"So what service did you render?"

Louie kissed Coceaux on the nose. "Rescued a damsel in distress. It's my specialty."

Coceaux extended and waved her free arm. "Who are all these people?"

"Oh, Avery's friends and relatives. And the neighbors."

"These are your neighbors?" asked Coceaux.

"Yep."

"They're all crazy."

Louie grinned at her. "That they are."

Tha-tha-tha-that's all folks!

Just Off the Streetcar Line

ABOUT THE AUTHOR

The author cannot imagine why the public would want to know anything about her, as her life pales next to the lives of such luminaries as Bennifer, Angelina, Brad and Britney, but here goes:

The author is a native New Orleanian.
The author is a Native American.
The author's husband is a Native American blacksmith and organic gardner.
The author's son is a Jewish poet (we're a multi-faceted American family).
The author is an uptown urban animal.
The author lives with two wonderful feline friends and various forms of wildlife that crawl under the back door, all urban animals of dubious lineage.
The author survived her college years and her subsequent 20's primarily on a well-rounded diet of donuts, sangria, Blue Nun, Michelob, Jack-in-the-Box supertacos, pizza and pot. (Shocking! A college student who smokes pot, drinks cheap booze, and eats junk food!)
The author's father was a rocket scientist (for real).
The author's mother was a home economics teacher (an extinct species from what I hear).
The author deeply regrets the 80's, her second marriage, several boyfriends and underwire bras.
The author has been accused of being an alien.
The author is tired of talking about herself and besides, the mother ship is waiting.

Just Off the Streetcar Line